BestMasters

Springer awards „BestMasters" to the best master's theses which have been completed at renowned universities in Germany, Austria, and Switzerland.
The studies received highest marks and were recommended for publication by supervisors. They address current issues from various fields of research in natural sciences, psychology, technology, and economics.
The series addresses practitioners as well as scientists and, in particular, offers guidance for early stage researchers.

Michael Haba

The Case of State Liability

20 Years after Francovich

With a foreword by Dr. Markus Frischhut

Springer Gabler

Michael Haba
Vienna, Austria

BestMasters
ISBN 978-3-658-08079-2 ISBN 978-3-658-08080-8 (eBook)
DOI 10.1007/978-3-658-08080-8

Library of Congress Control Number: 2014955149

Springer Gabler

Printed on acid-free paper

Springer Gabler is a brand of Springer Fachmedien Wiesbaden
Springer Fachmedien Wiesbaden is part of Springer Science+Business Media
(www.springer.com)

Foreword

Over the years, the European Court of Justice (ECJ) has developed several seminal principles of the law of the European Union (EU), amongst others the principle of State Liability. The practical relevance of "a new legal order of international law" very much depends on two questions: First, if rights are directly attributable to individuals (this includes citizens as well as companies), and second, if breaches of EU law are efficaciously sanctioned.

In many cases, EU law is not applied by the EU itself, but by single Member States, which from time to time find themselves between a rock and a hard place when they have to decide between complying with the duty of loyal cooperation and enforcing their own national interests. A good exemplification of the fact is this principle of State Liability, a liability for loss and damage caused to individuals as a result of breaches of European Union law for which the State can be held responsible.

Now, nearly 20 years after the leading case in this field (*Francovich and others vs. Italian Republic*), Michael Haba strives to analyse the principle of State Liability by means of chronological review, highlighting the different stages that turn-by-turn expanded this important principle.

The thesis at hand is structured chronologically in order to point out the development of this case-law driven principle. Although the *Francovich* case is seen as the founding stone of State Liability, the author takes a broader view to the matter and also includes the pre-Francovich starting points (chapter 2). The work then continues with the leading cases of *Francovich* (chapter 3), *Brasserie du Pêcheur* (chapter 4, 5 respectively) and *Köbler* (chapter 6). At the end, the author again takes a more extensive approach as he compares the principle of State Liability to the new line of compensation of damages (private enforcement) in EU competition law (chapter 7).

Overall Michael Haba not only displays a thorough effort by having analysed around 120 judgements, as well as relevant literature and other key documents, but also by having visualised the main findings in a very reader friendly way: He presents his findings step-by-step, each accompanied by respective illustrations (cumulating in an overall visual summary in Figure 6), and proves further user-friendliness by way of reference tables of case-law (both numerical and alphabetical), as well as relevant primary and secondary EU law in the appendices.

In closing I am confident that readers will find the oeuvre of Michael Haba, which provides them with both accessible and thorough information in the subject, as enjoyable as I did.

Dr. Markus Frischhut

Institutional Profile
MCI Management Center Innsbruck

Management Center Innsbruck (MCI) is an integral part of the unique "Comprehensive University Innsbruck" concept in Austria and has attained a leading position in international higher education as a result of its on-going quality and customer orientation. In the meantime 3,000 students, 1,000 faculty members, 200 partner universities worldwide and numerous graduates and employers appreciate the qualities of the Entrepreneurial School®.

MCI offers graduate, non-graduate and post-graduate educational programs of the highest standard to senior and junior managers from all management levels and branches. MCI's programs focus on all levels of the personality and include areas of state-of-the-art knowledge from science and practice relevant to business and society.

A wide range of Bachelor and Master study programs in the fields of management & society, technology & life sciences are offered. Curricula with a strong practical orientation, an international faculty and student body, the limited numbers of places, an optional semester abroad and internships with prestigious companies are among the many attractions of an MCI study program.

Embedded in a broad network of patrons, sponsors and partners, MCI is an important engine in the positioning of Innsbruck, Tyrol and Austria as a center for academic and international encounters. Our neighborly co-operation with the University of Innsbruck, the closeness to the lively Innsbruck Old Town and the powerful architecture of the location are an expression of the philosophy and the mission of this internationally exemplary higher education center.

www.mci.edu

Abstract

This thesis analyzes the principle of Member State Liability, which provides a general right to damages whenever the rule of EU law is infringed by Member States and its authorities. The paper, through literary research, ascertains that the doctrine evolved through three stages until becoming the unified approach that it is today. The author subsequently examines whether a fourth stage can be established. It is emphasized that the principle's foundations lay at the outset of the EEC, when the Court sought means to foster the enforcement of EC law. With no legal basis in the Treaty, it turned to its case law to create the precursor of the principle while relying on the cooperation of national courts. Due to lack of uniformity of this approach, the ECJ was required to bring a right to damages under EC law. It is stated that the Court introduced the general principle of State Liability in *Francovich*. It lay down the substantive aspects required to incur liability of the State with regard to non-transposition of directives, but it left the procedural aspects to national courts under the principles of effectiveness and equivalence. As the ruling gave little guidance regarding the application of the principle, more clarification and development was needed. It is highlighted that these matters were resolved in *Brasserie/Factortame III*, which emphasized the universality of the principle by introducing the sufficiently serious breach criterion in light of which liability for any type of breach by Member States could be assessed. This culpability test proved to be ambiguous, resulting in inconsistency. It is ascertained that in following case law the Court clarified the conditions of State Liability, but also revised the sufficiently serious breach criterion and analyzed the compatibility of national laws. It is stated that the ECJ expanded the principle in the case of *Köbler*, extending liability of the State to breaches of EC law by last instance courts. It limited the universality of the doctrine by requiring a manifest infringement in such cases. It is presented that in a series of cases stemming from breaches of directly effective competition rules of EC law, the Court was prompted to rule whether these rules afforded individuals with a right to reparation, and whether this could be rooted in the *Francovich* principle. It is concluded that the ECJ confirmed the former, but regarding the latter it did not refer to the right of damages under EC law, meaning that no fourth stage in the evolution of the State Liability principle was precipitated.

Table of Contents

Table of Figures

Table of Abbreviations

AG	Advocate General
Art. (Arts.)	Article (Articles)
BSE	Bovine spongiform encephalopathy
cf.	confer
e.g.	*exempli gratia* (for example)
EC	European Community
EC Bull supp	Bulletin of the European Communities, supplement
ECHR	European Convention for the Protection of Human Rights and Fundamental Freedoms
ECJ	European Court of Justice
ECR	European Court Reports
ECSC	European Coal and Steel Community
ECtHR	European Court of Human Rights
EEC	European Economic Community
et seqq.	*et sequens* (and the following)
EU	European Union
icw.	in conjunction with
Ltd	limited (company with limited liability under UK law)
OJ	Official Journal of the European Union
p. (pp.)	page (pages)
para (paras)	paragraph (paragraphs)
plc	public limited company (under UK law)
SA	Société Anonyme (public limited company under French law)
SLSI	special length-of-service increment
SpA	Società per azioni (public limited company under Italian law)
TEC	Treaty establishing the European Community
TEU	Treaty on European Union
TFEU	Treaty on the Functioning of the European Union

1 Introduction

1.1 Problem Definition

More than 20 years have passed since the case of *Andrea Francovich and Danila Bonifaci & Others v. Italian Republic*[1] where the European Court of Justice (ECJ) laid down the principle of Member State liability for the very first time.[2] Such a development was quite revolutionary, because State liability, in particular for legislative or judicial breaches, was still an infrequent phenomenon in most European jurisdictions.[3] In fact, an individual seeking claims for damages sustained by State authorities could only rely upon national laws, which at the time were not consistent.[4]

The initial spark for this development dates back to the early and seminal case of *Van Gend en Loos v. Netherlands Inland Revenue Administration.*[5] Fifty years ago, in 1963, the Court established the principle of direct effect and pronounced the private enforceability of Community law in addition to the public enforcement regime explicitly provided in the Treaty of Rome.[6] However, the principle of direct effect could only offer judicial relief to individuals in specific cases while denying rights to damages in others. The introduction of the general principle of Member State liability in *Francovich* resolved this potential deficit, providing that under certain conditions "governments of Member States must make good any damage suffered by individuals (...) resulting from any act or omission imputed to a branch of the government which turns out to be inconsistent with Community law"[7].[8]

Still, while *Francovich* succeeded in remedying deficits of existing weaknesses, it left many questions unanswered and introduced even more.[9] What followed was a first generation of cases in which the Court established the legal basis of Member State liability as well as the conditions according to which a right to reparation arose.[10] In 1996, the principle of Member State liability was further clarified and extended in the joined cases of *Brasserie du Pêcheur SA v. Ger-*

---

1 Joined Cases C-6/90 and C-9/90 *Andrea Francovich and Danila Bonifaci & Others v. Italian Republic (Francovich)* [1991] ECR I-5357.
2 Cf. Tallberg, 2000, p. 110.
3 Cf. Granger, 2007, p. 1.
4 Cf. Vaitkevičiūtė, 2011, p. 63.
5 Case 26/62 *Van Gend en Loos v. Netherlands Inland Revenue Administration (Van Gend en Loos)* [1963] ECR 1.
6 Cf. Betlem, 2005, p. 139.
7 Caranta, 1993, p. 277.
8 Cf. ibid.
9 Cf. Tallberg, 2000, p. 110.
10 Cf. Tridimas, 2001, p. 302.

many and *The Queen v. Secretary of State for Transport, ex parte Factortame Ltd & Others*[11] where the ECJ held that it was applicable to all breaches of Community law irrespective of which branch of government they originated from and without regard to direct effect of the Community provisions.[12] In light of this the Court revised the conditions under which the State and its organs could be liable in damages for breaches of Community law.[13] It was issues arising from putting this new policy into practice which led to a second generation of cases where the emphasis lay on establishing liability under these refined conditions.[14]

What followed was a third generation in the progressive development of the *Francovich*-line of cases, where Member State liability was extended to apply, not only to unlawful acts of the legislature and administration, but also to judicial breaches of Community law. In the seminal case of *Gerhard Köbler v. Austria*,[15] the Court first held that the principle of Member State liability also had a bearing on unlawful acts of national courts adjudicating at last instance.[16]

By looking back at the history of cases it can be established that the case law in relation to the principle of Member State liability has developed quite uniquely. In the beginning the Court took little notice of the legal remedies conferred upon individuals by Community law, while in the later stages of development it took an active role in matters regarding the conditions under which the safeguarding of rights was ensured by the courts of the Member States.[17]

Now, more than 20 years after *Francovich*, the substantial number of judgments by the Court gives occasion to analyze old and new aspects of the principle of Member State liability by revisiting old cases, and by introducing new ones, which have not been in the limelight of existing legal publications.

1.2 Objectives and Research Questions

This thesis seeks to analyze, by means of critically discussing the evolution of case law, the principle of Member State liability for an infringement of European Union law. In order to achieve this objective, it shall explore the cases that gave rise to the judgment in *Francovich* and those that followed, and perform a

---

11 Joined Cases C-46/93 and C-48/93 *Brasserie du Pêcheur SA v. Germany and The Queen v. Secretary of State for Transport, ex parte Factortame Ltd. & Others (Brasserie/Factortame III)* [1996] ECR I-1029.

12 Cf. Tallberg, 2000, p. 110.

13 Cf. ibid.

14 Cf. Kapteyn & VerLoren van Themaat, 2008, p. 559.

15 Case C-224/01 *Gerhard Köbler v. Austria (Köbler)* [2003] ECR I-10239.

16 Cf. Scherr, 2012, p. 566.

17 Cf. Caranta, 1993, p. 279.

chronological review highlighting the stages, which expanded the principle of State liability.[18] As a result, both the past developments and the future directions of case law on non-contractual liability of the Member States will be addressed.

This assessment shall also illustrate how the *Francovich* principle operates in the legal order of the European Union. For that purpose, the paper aims at, *inter alia*, explaining what the substantive scope of application of the principle is, what the conditions for incurring liability of the State are and what constitutes an infringement of Union law. The examination will provide details on the effects the principle has on the enforcement of Union law, especially when it comes to directives, and how it is interconnected with the judicial protection of individual rights.

The paper shall include, but not be limited to, the landmark case of *Francovich*, which constituted the first stage, the *Brasserie/Factortame III* judgment, which introduced the second stage, and the case of *Köbler*, which many law scholars see as giving rise to the third stage. After giving an overview of the existing stages of development, the paper shall determine, by taking into account a new generation of cases, whether a fourth stage in the evolution of State liability can be established.

The paper shall provide the reader with a complete, but not exhaustive understanding of the principle of Member State liability in European Union law. Accordingly, it shall not deal in any part with non-contractual liability of the European Union purely for its own cause. The thesis shall focus on seminal decisions by the Court and include the most relevant cases in its examination. However, it shall not focus on judgments of national courts of the Member States in State liability cases as its own motive. Neither shall it discuss the jurisprudential implications of State liability on Member States.

1.3 Methodology and Intended Research Methods

The Master thesis shall be based on theoretical research. The goals and research questions defined in the previous chapter shall be answered by means of thorough literary research carried out on available legal publications, scientific documents, databases of law, and judgments of the Court, all pertaining to the topic.

---

18 Cf. Aalto, 2011, pp. 2-3.

The thesis is structured in eight chapters: The **first chapter** provides the reader with a brief introduction to the subject matter of Member State liability in European Union law. It establishes the background of the paper by roughly outlining the development of the principle over time. Against that background, it defines the objectives and the methodology of the paper.

In the **second chapter**, the beginnings of the principle of Member State liability are illustrated. First through reference to the origins of the early foundations rooted in both the Treaties and general principles. Then through a description of the evolution of early case law based on these foundations.

The **third chapter** examines the inauguration of the principle of State liability in the seminal case of *Francovich.*[19] First, it reviews the circumstances of the case, describing how the case came into being and what the underlying problems faced by the Court were. Turning to the judgment, it discusses the rationale of the Court in establishing liability of the State and provides a detailed account of the conditions necessary for incurring such liability.

In the **fourth chapter**, the clarification and extension of the *Francovich* principle in the case of *Brasserie/Factortame III*[20] is discussed. After providing background information on the case, the chapter addresses the decision of the Court. In the course of this, revisiting the conditions for liability as revised by the judgment, and introducing the new requirement of a sufficiently serious breach. Subsequently, it discusses the remaining issues pertaining to the judgment.

The **fifth chapter** revolves around the cases that came into existence after *Brasserie/Factortame III.* In that context, it focuses on the significant decisions of the Court in the time period from 1996 up to 2013. Thereby, it classifies the case law according to three categories, all in relation to the conditions of liability: firstly, decisions leading to further clarification of the requirements, secondly, rulings leading to deference to national courts, and lastly, those pertaining to the aspect of the compatibility of national laws. Notably, the chapter does not involve landmark decisions; these are addressed in their own respective chapters.

In the **sixth chapter**, the extension of the principle of State liability to judicial breaches of last instance courts is discussed. To begin with, the seminal case of *Köbler v. Austria*,[21] which first raised the issue, is presented. After providing facts on the case, the chapter addresses the judgment of the Court, with putting

---

19 *Francovich* (fn 1).
20 *Brasserie/Factortame III* (fn 11).
21 *Köbler* (fn 15).

special emphasis on how liability of the State includes wrongful acts of the judiciary while safeguarding the principle of judicial independence. The chapter concludes with a discussion of subsequent jurisprudence, which acted as an affirmation of such liability.

The **seventh chapter** introduces the subject of liability for individuals for breaches of Community law. It illustrates that the legal order of the Community can place duties on individuals and addresses whether these duties can incur liability upon individuals for damages occasioned by them. It focuses on the prominent judgments pertaining to the competition law regime of the Community. By referring to the opinions of prominent academic researchers and legal practitioners, it establishes if such liability is only restricted to the field of competition law, or can be construed as an extension of the general principle of State liability.

In the final and **eighth chapter**, a summary of the paper is presented and the most relevant results of the literary research are highlighted.

Please note that in the appendices, for the comfort and convenience of the reader, tables referencing all cases and legislation mentioned in the paper are provided. All legal references, if cited in full in the text, are subsequently cited in short whereas reference to the full citation is provided. If they are cited in the footnotes, they are only cited in short in the same chapter and again cited in full on their next occurrence. All references to Treaty articles are references to the numbering of the respective Treaty in effect during the pertaining time period, in addition a reference to subsequent Treaties is provided in square brackets.

2 State Liability in Damages Before Francovich

2.1 Foundations of State Liability in Community Law

One of the prominent challenges for the European Economic Community (EEC) at its outset, as it is for the European Union today,[22] was the act of compelling compliance with its directives.[23] It was well established that "[a] directive shall be binding, as to the result to be achieved, upon each Member State to which it is addressed, but shall leave to the national authorities the choice of form and methods".[24] The failure to transpose directives within specified time periods or transposition that was not efficient, such as incomplete or incorrect transposition, was one of the most significant problems in the legal order of the Community.[25]

2.1.1 Duty of Sincere Cooperation

Member States were obliged under Art. 5 EEC [*ex Art. 10 TEC; now Art. 4(3) TEU*] to take any actions that were best suited to comply with their obligations under Community law. Moreover, the same Treaty article specified that they had to refrain from any actions that would compromise the fulfillment of these responsibilities.[26] The obligations under Art. 5 EEC were dependent on, and might be invoked together with, either primary or secondary Community law.[27] For example, a Member State could violate its obligations toward the Community, if it did not comply with provisions of the Treaty, did not give effect to regulations, or did not transpose directives or decisions into its national legal system.[28]

2.1.2 Infringement Proceedings

When a Member State was considered to be in default of Treaty obligations, the Commission was entitled to bring action against it before the Court under the infringement procedure laid down by Art. 169 EEC [*ex Art. 226 TEC; now Art. 258 TFEU*].[29] On that account it was solely for the ECJ to assess whether or not the Member State was in default:

---

22 Cf. Conant, 2012, pp. 27-28.
23 Cf. Hanft, 1991, p. 1237.
24 Art. 189(3) EEC [*ex Art. 249(3) TEC; now Art. 288(3) TFEU*].
25 Cf. Prechal, 2006, p. 7.
26 Cf. Art. 5 EEC [*ex Art. 10 TEC; now Art. 4(3) TEU*].
27 Cf. Case 2/73 *Geddo v. Ente Nazionale Risi (Geddo)* [1973] ECR 865, p. 878.
28 Cf. Art. 189(3) EEC *icw.* Art. 5 EEC.
29 Cf. Art. 169 EEC [*ex Art. 226 TEC; now Art. 258 TFEU*].

> If the Court of Justice finds that a Member State has failed to fulfil an obligation under [the] Treaty [establishing the European Economic Community], the State shall be required to take the necessary measures to comply with the judgment of the Court.[30]

It is understood that these provisions of public enforcement, in terms of infringement procedures, compelled disobedient Member States to fulfill their obligations under Community law.[31] Although these proceedings were frequently put into effect, their ramifications, however, were deemed to be marginal, because an insubordinate Member State could refrain from complying with the judgment,[32] for example, by opting for a route of formal, minimalistic compliance.[33] The power of infringement proceedings was substantially constrained by the fact that they only led to a declaratory judgment. Moreover, prior to the coming into effect of the Maastricht Treaty, which established financial sanctions, the infringement procedure depended on the risk of public shaming to compel Member States to abide with Community law.[34] As a consequence, Member States might not comply with their obligation under Art. 171(1) EEC [*ex Art. 228(1) TEC; now Art. 260(1) TFEU*] to remedy the breach of Community law.[35]

In fact such non-compliance of Member States posed a clear and present danger to not only the success of the new legal order of the Community, but also to the unified exercise of Community law, to the extent that the survival of the Community was at stake. Without loyal cooperation, guaranteeing the full observance with Community law by all Member States, the Community would have only marginal chances of survival.[36] Consequently, it was up to the Court, whose responsibility it is to make sure that "the law is observed",[37] "to maximise the effective enforcement of Community law by judicial means".[38] As a result, it successively adopted measures to minimize the effects of failure to comply with Community laws by the Member States.[39] Consequently, the ECJ took the spirited initiative of authorizing the private enforcement of Community laws.[40]

---

30 Art. 171(1) EEC [*ex Art. 228(1) TEC; now Art. 260(1) TFEU*].
31 Cf. Hanft, 1991, pp. 1239-1240.
32 Cf. ibid, p. 1237.
33 Cf. Conant, 2012, p. 28.
34 Cf. Kelemen, 2004, pp. 41-42.
35 Cf. Lock, 2012, p. 1677.
36 Cf. Steiner, 1993, p. 4.
37 Art. 164 EEC [*ex Art. 220(1) TEC; now Art. 19(1) TEU*].
38 Cf. Steiner, 1993, p. 5.
39 Cf. Hanft, 1991, p. 1238.
40 Cf. Craig & de Búrca, 2011, p. 181.

2.1.3 Judicial Protection of Individual Rights

The Court assumed that fostering a smooth operation of the Community altogether implied safeguarding the conformity of the Member States with their duties.[41] It realized right from the start the importance of the role which individuals could assume,[42] pointing out in *Van Gend en Loos*,[43] that "[t]he vigilance of individuals concerned to protect their rights amounts to an effective supervision in addition to the supervision entrusted by Arts. 169 and 170 EEC [*ex Arts. 226-227 TEC; now Arts. 258-259 TFEU*] to the diligence of the Commission and of the Member States".[44] Even though these procedures only conferred standing upon the Commission and Member States, the ECJ had given the articles of the Treaty a broad interpretation as to uphold the full effectiveness of Community law,[45] creating significant means through which rights of individuals could be enforced.[46] In that respect the Court implied that in spite of the fact that individuals had not been given standing under these provisions, it did not preclude them from claiming that a Member State had violated its obligations under Community law before national courts, which might in turn question the ECJ on the interpretation of Community law pertaining to the respective issue. In doing so, individuals would invoke their rights afforded by Community law before national courts,[47] which worked side by side with the Court, in form of a judicial cooperation, with the goal of making sure that Community law was enacted in a uniform manner in all the Member States.[48] Accordingly, by endorsing the rights of individuals, the ECJ was able to foster compliance by the Member States with their obligations under Community law.[49]

2.1.4 Direct Effect of Community Law

In *Van Gend en Loos,* the Court introduced the principle of direct effect that set out the basis for the individual private enforcement of Community rights by modifying the legal status of individuals.[50] Thus, it ruled that an article of the Treaty gave rise to rights that might be exercised before national courts by individual legal subjects.[51] Moreover, it emphasized that these rights did not only

41 Cf. Arnull, 2000, p. 188.
42 Cf. ibid.
43 *Van Gend en Loos* (fn 5).
44 Ibid, p. 13.
45 Cf. Hanft, 1991, pp. 1239-1240.
46 Cf. De Witte, 2011, p. 359.
47 Cf. Lenaerts & Van Nuffel, 2011, pp. 20-21.
48 Cf. Case 16/65 *Firma G. Schwarze v. Einfuhr- und Vorratsstelle für Getreide und Futtermittel (Schwarze)* [1965] ECR 877, p. 886.
49 Cf. Arnull, 2000, p. 188.
50 Cf. Craig & de Búrca, 2011, p. 181.
51 Cf. *Van Gend en Loos* (fn 5), p. 12.

emerge where they were explicitly established by Treaty provisions, but additionally on grounds of duties that the Treaty laid down.[52] As a result, not only Treaty provisions, but also provisions established in acts by the institutions of the Community might confer rights upon individuals.[53]

Consequently, by scrutinizing the subject matter and the phrasing pertaining to Art. 12 EEC [*ex Art. 25 TEC; now Art. 30 TFEU*], which posed a central issue in *Van Gend en Loos*, the Court determined the requirements for direct effect: a provision must be clear, unconditional and not depend on any further intervention by the Member States.[54] Therefore a provision has direct effect where the ECJ has the authority, without having to resort to additional measures of implementation, to arrive at a judicial interpretation in a case, as a consequence of which individual legal subjects might obtain rights flowing from that provision.[55]

Furthermore, applying similar rationale as in *Van Gend en Loos*, the Court advanced the principle of direct effect, in the course adapting it to be also applicable in cases where directives had not been implemented or had been implemented incorrectly, but for which the time frame for transposition into national law had elapsed.[56]

In *Van Duyn v. Home Office*,[57] the ECJ placed reliance on the principle of effectiveness and established that it was the binding character of directives that constituted the direct effect of their provisions.[58] It held that according to Art. 189 EEC [*ex Art. 249 TEC; now Art. 288 TFEU*] both regulations and directives were capable of having direct effect. When it came to directives, it continued to observe that denying individuals the right to rely on such acts would, firstly, be irreconcilable with the binding effect assigned to directives, and secondly, significantly impair the usefulness of the acts.[59] In *Becker v. Finanzamt Münster-Innenstadt*,[60] the Court determined that a Member State is prohibited from gaining an advantage from its own non-fulfillment of an obligation under Community law.[61] It ruled that individuals were not precluded from relying on provisions by direct effective directives in the event that a Member State had failed to transpose the directive into its domestic legal system within the specified time limit.[62]

---

52 Cf. ibid.
53 Cf. Lenaerts & Van Nuffel, 2011, pp. 811-812.
54 Cf. *Gend en Loos* (fn 5), p. 13.
55 Cf. Lenaerts & Van Nuffel, 2011, p. 810.
56 Cf. Hanft, 1991, p. 1246.
57 Case 41/74 *Yvonne van Duyn v. Home Office (Van Duyn)* [1974] ECR 1337.
58 Cf. Prechal, 1990, p. 452.
59 Cf. Van *Duyn* (fn 57), para 12.
60 Case 8/81 *Ursula Becker v. Finanzamt Münster-Innenstadt (Becker)* [1982] ECR 53.
61 Cf. Prechal, 1990, p. 453.
62 Cf. *Becker* (fn 60), paras 23-25.

And in *Marshall v. Southampton and South West Hampshire Area Health Authority*,[63] the ECJ established that directives did not have horizontal direct effect by holding that

> the binding nature of directives, which constitutes the basis for the possibility of relying on the directive before a national court, exists only in relation to 'each Member State to which it is addressed'. It follows that a directive may not of itself impose obligations on an individual and that a provision of a directive may not be relied upon as such against such a person.[64]

Although the Court went to great length in developing its jurisprudence on direct effect, it did not explicitly touch upon the subject of recovery of damages for individuals.[65] As a consequence, before the judgment of the ECJ in *Francovich*,[66] there was no direct legal relief obtainable for individuals in the event that a Member State failed to transpose a directive which was not directly effective. The Court had given direct effect to directives under the conditions that the directive was clear, precise and unconditional. However, if the directive did not fulfill these criteria, it could not have direct effect. Consequently, an individual who suffered loss and damage in the case of a failure by a Member State to transpose such a directive would remain without a direct remedy.[67] The only fallback for an individual at the time was to ask the Commission to initiate a public infringement proceeding according to Art. 169 EEC against the Member State that was in breach of its obligations under Community law.[68]

2.2 In Search of a Legal Basis for State Liability

A Member State could commit an infringement of Community law, for instance, by either entirely failing to transpose or incorrectly transposing the directive into its national legal system. An individual who suffered loss and damage by this or any other infringement of Community law should be entitled to make a claim for recovery of damages against the respective Member State before its national courts. However, cases pertaining to liability for damages involving directives had another extent. Firstly, to be effective, directives as legal instruments of Community law without direct applicability needed further implementation by

---

63 Case 152/84 *Marshall v. Southampton and South West Hampshire Area Health Authority (Marshall I)* [1986] ECR 723.
64 Ibid, para 48.
65 Cf. Hanft, 1991, p. 1238.
66 *Francovich* (fn 1).
67 Cf. Hanft, 1991, pp. 1266-1268.
68 Cf. ibid, p. 1247.

national authorities in the domestic legal systems of the Member States. And as pointed out previously, non-transposition or incorrect transposition of directives constituted a common problem in the early stages of the Community. Secondly, the preclusion of horizontal direct effect of directives presented further difficulties to both enforcement of Community law and effective judicial protection of individual rights. Both were issues that might be alleviated to a specific degree by the application of legal remedies.[69]

Indeed, the belief that an imputable breach of Community law by a Member State should in turn provide grounds for remedial action under national laws on public non-contractual liability was not a novel idea.[70] For some time the eventuality had been considered that Member States had to provide remedy for damages.[71] For example, in 1975, the Court, in a supplement to the Bulletin of the European Communities, pertaining to the establishment of a 'European Union', recommended that "the safeguarding of [individual] rights presupposes that in the event of a failure by a state to fulfill an obligation, persons adversely affected thereby may obtain redress before their national courts"[72].[73] Moreover, before the decision of the ECJ in *Francovich*, there had been an attempt by the Commission to amend the Treaty on European Union, while it was being drafted, to include a stipulation on the recovery of damages.[74] However, in the end no such stipulations were established in the Treaty, and the issue was left to be governed in its entirety by the domestic laws of the Member States leading to distinct differences in both methodology and results. As a consequence, in that time period both academia and judicial practice were diligently in search of a legal basis under the legal order of the Community to surpass the obstacles in national regimes of non-contractual liability in the legal systems of the Member States. The jurisprudence of the Court played an important role in the attainment of this objective.[75]

2.2.1 First Declaration of State Liability

In 1960, early proclamations of State liability in damages were first made in case law on the European Coal and Steel Community (ECSC) Treaty.[76] It was in *Jean-E. Humblet v. Belgium,*[77] a case concerning the tax immunity of ECSC

69 Cf. Prechal, 2006, p. 271.
70 Cf. ibid.
71 Cf. Steiner, 1993, p. 7.
72 EC Bull supp 9/75, p. 18.
73 Cf. ibid.
74 Cf. EC Bull supp 2/91, pp. 152-153.
75 Cf. Prechal, 2006, pp. 271-272.
76 Cf. Douglas-Scott, 2002, p. 321.
77 Case 6/60 *Jean-E. Humblet v. Belgium (Humblet)* [1960] ECR 559.

civil servants, where the Court ruled, on the basis of Art. 86 ECSC, that a Member State is under an obligation to annul a legislative or administrative act by a national authority that is contrary to Community law as well as to provide indemnification to private parties for any repercussions that may have been brought on by such an illegitimate act.[78]

In spite of the fact that the judgment of the ECJ was held under the ECSC Treaty, it was also applicable to the EEC Treaty, because Art. 86 ECSC was almost equivalent to Art. 5 EEC. Another important aspect in the case was that the Court laid down the extent of its own jurisdiction.[79] Community law, on the grounds of the principle of separation of powers, did not confer upon the institutions of the Community the right to directly intervene in legislative or administrative matters of the Member States. Therefore, in cases of non-compliance with the Treaties, it remained the sole responsibility of the national jurisdictions of the Member State to decide on effective measures to observe the judgment handed down by the ECJ.[80] In the event of a national provision infringing Community law, the revocation of such a provision by national courts of a Member State might constitute a sufficiently effective legal relief. However, many cases were not all that clear-cut, because violations of Community law by Member States were not always made up of provisions which the national courts could simply revoke. For example, there might be actions carried out by the State itself in which the national courts were not involved at all. Furthermore, not all national jurisdictions empowered their nationals to bring actions for damages against the State for its violation of Community law.[81]

According to Barav, there was arguable authority in the ruling by the Court in *Humblet* that the right to reparation in the national legal systems arose as a consequence of a judgment by the ECJ under Arts. 169 to 171 EEC.[82] Therefore, the ruling, acting as a point of departure, should provide further authority in light of recovery for damages due to infringement of Community law for the cases to follow.[83]

2.2.2 Early Recognition of State Liability

Twelve years later and in the ambit of the European Economic Community (EEC) followed *Commission v. Italy*,[84] a case concerning premiums for slaugh-

---

78 Cf. ibid, p. 569.
79 Cf. Barav, 1988, p. 152.
80 Cf. *Humblet* (fn 77), pp. 568-569.
81 Cf. Schermers & Waelbroeck, 2001, p. 204.
82 Cf. Barav, 1988, p. 152.
83 Cf. Prechal, 2006, p. 273.
84 Case 39/72 *Commission v. Italy (Slaughtered Cows)* [1973] ECR 101.

tering cows, where the Court shifted from its previous approach pertaining to a violation of Community laws laid down in *Humblet*, and "recognized the non-contractual liability of the Member States without specifying its legal basis"[85]. The ECJ held that

> in the face of both a delay in the performance of an obligation and a definite refusal, a judgment by the Court under Articles 169 and 171 of the Treaty may be of substantive interest as establishing the basis of a responsibility that a Member State can incur as a result of its default, as regards other Member States, the Community or private parties.[86]

In its ruling, the Court clarified that a judgment, according to Art. 169 and 171 EEC, establishing a violation of Community law, might act as a basis of liability that a Member State might become subject to under its own rules of national law as a consequence of its imputable violation of individual rights.[87]

Prechal put forward that it could be reasoned from the ruling of the ECJ in *Slaughtered Cows* that liability of the State could be based not just on infringement proceedings. In her view, if it followed from a reference for a preliminary ruling that a Member State was in default of its obligation to transpose a directive or incorrectly transposed a directive, then a private party, who was precluded to rely on the direct effect of directives, could also be entitled to bring action against the Member State, for example, for recovery of damages. However, the downside of any interpretation was that the outcome of this course still relied upon the existence of effective legal remedies under respective domestic laws.[88]

Yet, the official rationale of the Court behind the ruling was, according to AG Mischo in his opinion in *Francovich*,[89] that State liability might provide a partial remedy in circumstances where it was impossible for a Member State to belatedly perform its duties.[90] Moreover, he pointed out that the jurisprudence of the ECJ, up to that point, was not authoritative enough to provide a definite answer as regards the question of the principle of liability of Member States for imputable breaches of Community law.[91] Consequently, the Court in *Slaughtered*

---

85 Bebr, 1994, p. 328.
86 *Slaughtered Cows* (fn 84), para 11.
87 Cf. Tridimas, 1998, p. 12.
88 Cf. Prechal, 1990, p. 466.
89 Opinion of AG Mischo in Joined Cases C-6/90 and C-9/90 *Andrea Francovich and Danila Bonifaci & Others v. Italian Republic* [1991] ECR I-5357.
90 Cf. ibid, para 59.
91 Cf. ibid, para 57.

Cows did not give clear guidance whether the right to reparation was a matter to be determined only under national law or whether it was a subject of Community law. If the latter was the case then the opaque language used by the ECJ in the decision suggested that some sort of conditionality, which at that time was not introduced, had to still be established.[92]

2.2.3 Reliance on National Systems of Liability

Before the emergence of *Francovich*, case law of the Court on Member State liability for the breach of Community law was yet in a nascent state. After *Humblet* and *Slaughtered Cows* the circumstances were such that the ECJ acknowledged, on the basis of its previous jurisprudence, that a Member State was under the duty to make restitution for the breach of Community law. However, it did not specify how the injured party had to be compensated for a wrong sustained, consequently leaving aside all details in reference to the recovery of damages.[93] The reason for this course taken by the Court was not founded on any concerns on the principle of non-contractual liability of the Member States for an infringement of Community law, but rather on questions regarding the particular legal basis for such liability.[94] It was well understood that the right to reparation with respect to non-contractual liability was enacted in the legal systems of all the Member States. However, it was less clear whether a Member State could be held culpable for an infringement of Community law under the national regimes of public non-contractual liability and what the specific qualifications for assessing this culpability were.[95]

The ruling of the ECJ in *Russo v. AIMA,*[96] a case concerning "an infringement of a regulation on the common organization of agricultural markets",[97] explicitly addressed some of the previously disregarded details pertaining to the question of State liability.[98] The ECJ held that

> [i]t is for the national court to decide on the basis of the facts of each case whether an individual (...) has suffered (...) damage.[99] If such damage has been caused through an infringement of Community law the

[92] Cf. Prechal, 2006, p. 273.
[93] Cf. Vaitkevičiūtė, 2011, p. 51.
[94] Cf. Bebr, 1992, p. 572.
[95] Cf. Prechal, 2006, p. 274.
[96] Case 60/75 *Russo v. AIMA (Russo)* [1976] ECR 45.
[97] Opinion of AG Mischo in *Francovich* (fn 89), para 43.
[98] Cf. Prechal, 2006, p. 274.
[99] *Russo* (fn 96), para 8.

> State is liable to the injured party [for] the consequences in the context of the provisions of national law on the liability of the State.[100]

As a consequence this ruling required that the national legal systems of the Member States had to afford the protection from rights flowing from Community law.[101] However, the Court had already established such a duty in its previous judgment in *SpA Salgoil v. Italian Ministry of Foreign Trade*,[102] where it held that

> [such rules] require the authorities, and in particular the relevant courts of the Member States, to protect the interests of those persons subject to their jurisdiction who may be affected by any possible infringement of the said provisions, by ensuring for them *direct and immediate protection* of their interests.[103]

In *Russo*, the Court committed itself to a particular course of action, which emanated from the principle of effective judicial protection and had one crucial advantage in comparison to the previous approach: a claim for reparation was no longer subject to a decision of the ECJ made under the infringement procedure, which was only declaratory in character. Consequently, national courts were authorized to scrutinize, apart from requesting a preliminary reference from the Court, whether or not their respective Member States were in violation of Community law, because the rights, which individuals acquired from Community law, were conferred upon them by Community law itself.[104]

2.2.3.1 Period of Nonintervention: Reliance on General Principles

The decision in *Russo* hinted that the Court accepted that non-contractual liability was founded on Community law and it was solely within the ambit of national law to regulate the conditions of liability, such as the recovery of damages.[105] However, in the wake of the judgment, the approach of the ECJ of subjecting the conditions of liability to national law was criticized, because it was deemed neither an adequate nor a predictable solution.[106] Firstly, it required the existence of a national regime of public contractual liability and secondly, the national conditions for liability in the Member States were divergent leading to differing

---

100 Ibid, para 9.

101 Cf. Opinion of AG Mischo in Case 60/75 *Russo v. AIMA (Russo)* [1976] ECR 45, paras 37-39.

102 Case 13/68 *SpA Salgoil v. Italian Ministry of Foreign Trade (Salgoil)* [1968] ECR 453.

103 Ibid, pp. 462-463 (emphasis added).

104 Cf. Prechal, 1995, p. 310.

105 Cf. Prechal, 2006, p. 274.

106 Cf. Bebr, 1992, p. 572.

outcomes.[107] Subsequently in 1977, Millarg made remarks on the potential drawbacks of a German draft Act on State Liability, which precluded legislative action or omission from State liability where its illegality stemmed from a violation of provisions of Community law with direct effect. He cautioned with prescience that the Court would be inclined to close obvious gaps in the liability regimes of the Member States, which, according to him, put 'citizens of the common market' at a disadvantage, by developing a liability rule for Member States under Community law, based on the general principles of law of the Member States, by means of preliminary ruling.[108]

Indeed, rightfully so, although throughout the 1970s the Court was still reluctant to intervene in matters pertaining to the national legal systems of the Member States.[109] Therefore it can be established that the ECJ gave little thought to the objective of unity of effective judicial protection as between the Member States as long as they observed the principal prerequisites of effectiveness and equivalence.[110] As a matter of fact, case law pertaining to the principle of effective protection of individuals still had to fully emerge. The early approach of relative nonintervention was a consequence of the prevailing notion at that time that Community law essentially only concerned itself with substantive parts of law, whereas the procedural parts were perceived to be completely under the authority of the Member States.[111]

Nevertheless, the stringent domestic requirements of public non-contractual liability could in certain situations be waived or adjusted in attainment of the objectives of effectiveness or effective judicial protection.[112] In any case these principles warranted only a restricted exercise of influence by the Community on the domestic autonomy of the Member States in "the provision of remedies and procedural rules to govern the exercise of Treaty rights"[113]. Still, the Court, from time to time, took the opportunity to subject not only the substantive, but also the procedural conditions of State liability, as established by the national jurisdictions of the Member States, to certain requirements.[114] In 1976 the cases of *Rewe-Zentral AG v. Landwirtschaftskammer für das Saarland*,[115] and

---

107 Cf. Prechal, 2006, p. 274.
108 Cf. Millarg, 1977, pp. 225-226.
109 Cf. Dougan, 2012, p. 86.
110 Cf. Dougan, 2002, p. 167.
111 Cf. Caranta, 1993, p. 279.
112 Cf. Prechal, 2006, p. 274.
113 Dougan, 2002, p. 167.
114 Cf. ibid.
115 Case 33/76 *Rewe-Zentral AG v. Landwirtschaftskammer für das Saarland (Rewe)* [1976] ECR 1989.

Comet BV v. Produktschap voor Siergewassen[116] followed, where the ECJ, following its non-interventionist approach, ruled that it was left to the respective national jurisdictions of the Member States to decide on procedural issues pertaining to claims in reference to the safeguarding of rights conferred upon individuals by Community law. In addition, however, it drew up two requirements, which had to be respected by national courts, because they were under the obligation to allow for the exercise of rights conferred by Community law. In both cases, the Court avoided taking the authority to decide for national courts which remedial actions were needed to guarantee an effective judicial protection.[117] Firstly, the procedural issues established in such a case had to be no less favorable than those provided for related domestic actions, and secondly, in all circumstances it must be possible to exercise the remedial action granted.[118] Both decisions set out the general frame of reference to which the ECJ has resorted to, since that time, in dealing with matters pertaining to decentralized enforcement of Community law.[119] However, following cases made it necessary to establish more extensive requirements to cope with the increasing volume of Community law cases in the courts of the Member States.[120]

2.2.3.2 Period of Intervention: Securing Effectiveness and Uniformity of Community Rights

During the 1980s further development of case law was gaining momentum with the Court becoming increasingly more inclined to intervene in the domestic legal systems of the Member States to improve the effective protection of rights conferred by Community law.[121]

Initially, the ECJ would continue to take its previous principled stance pursuant to the procedural autonomy of Member States. In 1979 the Court revisited the question of recovery of damages in its judgment in *Granaria BV v. Hoofdproduktschap voor Akkerbouwprodukten,*[122] a case pertaining denatured skimmed-milk powder used as animal feedstuff. In the judgment the ECJ held that a question of reparation by a national authority in respect to losses incurred to individuals by the public agencies or servants of Member States due to a violation of Community law was not subject to the non-contractual liability of the Community under Art. 215 EEC [*ex Art. 288 TEC; now Art. 340 TFEU*] and

---

116 Case 45/76 *Comet BV v. Produktschap voor Siergewassen (Comet)* [1976] ECR 2043.
117 Cf. Caranta, 1995, p. 705.
118 Cf. *Comet* (fn 116), paras 12-17; cf. *Rewe* (fn 115), para 5; cf. Caranta, 1993, p. 279.
119 Cf. Dougan, 2011, p. 411.
120 Cf. Krümmel & D'Sa, 2009, p. 275.
121 Cf. Dougan, 2012, p. 86.
122 Case 101/78 *Granaria BV v. Hoofdproduktschap voor Akkerbouwprodukten (Granaria)* [1979] ECR 623.

therefore had to be resolved pursuant to national laws of the respective Member State.[123] Then in 1981, the Court elucidated a number of issues related to judicial relief and summarized the matter aptly in *Rewe-Handelsgesellschaft Nord mbH and Rewe-Markt Steffen v. Hauptzollamt Kiel,*[124] by expounding that "The Treaty (...) was not intended to create new remedies in the national courts to ensure the observance of Community law other than those already laid down by national law".[125]

However, in 1983, starting with *Amministrazione delle Finanze dello Stato v. SpA San Giorgio,*[126] the ECJ changed both its approach and language considerably when it came to judicial protection.[127] On the one hand it revisited its rulings in *Rewe* and *Comet,*[128] but on the other hand it also took the opportunity to expand on the duty of national courts to protect the exercise of rights conferred by Community law by stating that "[national laws] may not be so framed as to render *virtually impossible* the exercise of rights conferred by Community law".[129] By this decision the Court limited the national procedural autonomy of the Member States by the principle of effectiveness for the very first time.[130] Furthermore in *Bozzetti v. Invernizzi SpA,*[131] it referred to its previous decision in *Salgoil*, where it held, concerning arguments involving the rights of individuals emanating from Community law, that "it is for the legal system of each Member State to determine which court has jurisdiction"[132]. However, more significantly it added that "(...) at the same time the Member States are responsible for ensuring that those rights are *effectively* protected in each case"[133].[134]

Finally, in what is to be referred as a landmark judgment on the principle of effective judicial protection, the Court, in *The Queen v. Secretary of State for Transport, ex parte Factortame,*[135] impinged on the sphere of operation of remedies under national law. In the light of the English rule refusing an injunction

---

123 Cf. ibid, para 14.
124 Case 158/80 *Rewe-Handelsgesellschaft Nord mbH and Rewe-Markt Steffen v. Hauptzollamt Kiel* (*Rewe v. Hauptzollamt Kiel)* [1981] ECR 1805.
125 Ibid, para 44.
126 Case 199/82 *Amministrazione delle Finanze dello Stato v. SpA San Giorgio (San Giorgio)* [1983] ECR 3595.
127 Cf. Dougan, 2011, p. 413.
128 Cf. *San Giorgio* (fn 126), paras 12-18.
129 Ibid, para 12 (emphasis added).
130 Cf. Opinion AG Léger in Case C-5/94, *The Queen v. Ministry of Agriculture, Fisheries and Food, ex parte Hedley Lomas Ltd.* [1996] ECR I-2553, para 149.
131 Case 179/84 *Bozzetti v. Invernizzi SpA (Bozzetti)* [1985] ECR 2301.
132 *Salgoil* (fn 102), p. 463.
133 *Bozzetti* (fn 131), para 17 (emphasis added).
134 Cf. ibid.
135 Case C-213/89 *The Queen v. Secretary of State for Transport, ex parte Factortame Ltd & Others (Factortame I)* [1990] ECR I-2433.

against the Crown, the ECJ established, with little regard for the procedural autonomy of the Member States, that a national court was under the duty to disapply national rules which were the single source of conflict in precluding it "from granting interim relief in order to ensure the full effectiveness of the judgment to be given on the existence of the rights claimed under Community law"[136], which were allegedly violated by domestic provisions.[137] As the case involved a national legal system in which an injunction, in principle, was common, the Court did not perceive its judgment to require the enactment of binding interim legal remedies into systems in which these were not provided. Although, it might lead to a process of convergence, the intention of the ECJ with its judgment in *Factortame I* was neither to unify existing national laws nor to make another remedial action available before the national courts of the Member States.[138] Therefore, the Court did not go insofar as to set out the requirements under which preliminary relief had to be awarded under Community law.[139]

2.3 Concluding Observations

The decisions of the Court in many of the aforementioned cases illustrated that it, at this stage, acknowledged the general principles of Community law, such as the principle of effectiveness and the doctrine of direct effect, of being fully capable to attain the objective of safeguarding the rights of individuals conferred under the legal order of the Community. An overview on these measures is provided by Figure 1.[140] Consequently, the ECJ did not concern itself too much with procedural issues, such as the recovery of damages, and therefore was inclined to leave them, as pointed out by Caranta, "with almost complete indifference",[141] to the national courts of the Member States. Nevertheless, there were a few cases where the Court seized the opportunity to dabble in the procedural autonomy granted to Member States. Ultimately, however, the decisions in these cases had close to no bearing on the procedural laws of the Member States.[142] Because of these reasons it was not entirely clear-cut whether or not the duty to provide reparation was flowing from Community law. Moreover, because Community rules did not determine specific conditions for State liability and the own national regimes of public non-contractually liability of

136 Ibid, para 21.
137 Cf. Kapteyn & VerLoren van Themaat, 2008, p. 550.
138 Cf. Harlow, 2000, p. 80.
139 Cf. Kapteyn & VerLoren van Themaat, 2008, p. 550.
140 See Figure 1: Overview on the Enforcement Measures of the European Economic Community, p. 24.
141 Caranta, 1993, p. 279.
142 Cf. ibid.

the Member States were not consistent, no uniform right to reparation was provided in the domestic legal systems of the Member States.[143]

However, against the background of this situation the following problem arose: In spite of varying methods of affording provisions of Community law with direct or indirect effect, such an approach would not aid a plaintiff every time, because he might have sustained harm which could not be remedied by such means. Thus, the private enforcement of Community rights granted to individuals was not fully safeguarded by virtue of the direct or indirect effect stemming from rules of the legal order of the Community. As a result, it was imperative for the Court to establish further means of safeguarding individual rights by constituting the principle of liability of the Member States for violation of Community rules. This development was carried out in a variety of cases beginning with the landmark case of *Francovich* in 1991, where the ECJ affirmed that State liability was an inherent part of the legal order of the European Community.[144] Accordingly, it was the decision of the Court in *Francovich* that would put an end to the many questions raised as to the legal basis of State liability.[145]

143 Cf. Vaitkevičiūtė, 2011, p. 52.
144 Cf. Van Dam, 2013, p. 39.
145 Cf. Prechal, 2006, p. 275.

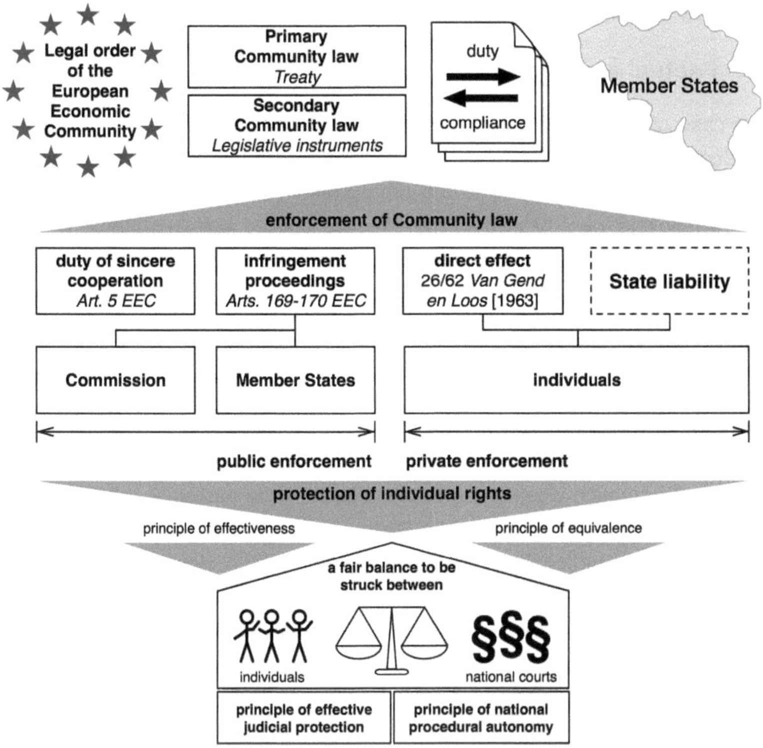

Figure 1: Overview on the Enforcement Measures of the European Economic Community

Figure 1. The measures which the then legal order of the EEC used to enforce its laws, compelling Member States to comply with their duties and safeguarding individual rights. First, methods of public enforcement were employed. Then, in the seminal judgment of *Van Gend en Loos*, the ECJ additionally established private enforcement in terms of the principle of direct effect. However, in practice, none of these measures were 100% effective. Problems arose particularly in the field of directives, where Member States frequently dismissed their obligation to implement them into national law and in the case of directives with no direct effect, even depriving individuals of their rights under EEC rules. As a consequence, it became important for the European Court to establish a right to damages under EEC law to make sure individuals and their rights were efficiently protected.

Source: Own compilation.

3 The Seminal Francovich Judgment on State Liability

3.1 Factual and Procedural Background

The case of *Francovich*[146] arose from the fact that Italy had been in breach of its Community obligation to implement Directive 80/987,[147] which unified domestic provisions pertaining to the protection of employees in the event that their employers went bankrupt. The directive obliged Member States to make necessary arrangements to ensure the payment of unsettled claims by employees arising from working contracts or employer-to-employee relationships.[148] For the accomplishment of this objective, the Member States had to setup guarantee institutions, which in turn had to be funded by the employers whilst being independent of them, and additionally not come under the control of their creditors.[149] The directive, while obliging the Member States to determine guarantee institutions which had to settle the claims, left the Member States with significant discretion when it came to establishing the particular procedures essential for attaining its goals.[150] The State of Italy ought to have transposed the directive into its national laws by 23. October 1983.[151] However, Italy did not heed its obligation to transpose the directive within the required time limit. Consequently, in *Commission v. Italy*,[152] the Commission initiated an infringement procedure against Italy under Art. 169 EEC [*ex Art. 226 TEC; now Art. 258 TFEU*]. In its judgment delivered on 2. February 1989, the Court held that Italy was indeed in breach of its Treaty obligations, because it had defaulted on the implementation of the directive within the time limit for transposition.[153]

In 1991, when the case of *Francovich* came before the ECJ, the State of Italy had still not adopted the necessary measures laid down by Art. 189 EEC [*ex Art. 249 TEC; now Art. 288 TFEU*], even though the time limit for transposition of Directive 80/987 into national law had long been expired, and it had already been found to be in violation of its Community obligation by the previous judgment of the Court in *Commission v. Italy*.[154] According to Bebr the circumstanc-

---

146 *Francovich* (fn 1).

147 Council Directive 80/987/EEC of 20 October 1980 on the approximation of the laws of the Member States relating to the protection of employees in the event of the insolvency of the employer (OJ 1980 L 283, p. 23), as repealed by Directive 2008/94/EC of the European Parliament and of the Council of 22 October 2008 on the protection of employees in the event of the insolvency of their employer (OJ 2008 L 283, pp. 36-42).

148 Cf. Hanft, 1991, p. 1258.

149 Cf. Hartley, 2008, p. 230.

150 Cf. Bebr, 1992, p. 558.

151 Cf. Council Directive 80/987/EEC (fn 147), art. 12.

152 Case 22/87 *Commission v. Italy* [1989] ECR 143.

153 Cf. Hanft, 1991, p. 1258.

154 Cf. Caranta, 1993, p. 277.

es of the case manifestly illustrated the intrinsic legal vulnerability of directives as legal instruments and the continuing difficulties that arose in their transposition into national law. He pointed out that the Member States seemed to have regarded directives as second-class measures of Community law with little or next to no obligating authority. Even in the event that the Court held that a Member State was in violation of its obligations under Community law the judgment, being declaratory in nature, was far from constituting a satisfactory legal remedy.[155]

The claimants, who consisted out of Andrea Francovich, Danila Bonifaci and 33 other employees, were owed back payments of wages by their former Italian employers.[156] The employers of the claimants were companies which had become bankrupt in the course of operation leaving wages and other work related benefits unsettled, with inadequate net worth to pay off the claims by the employees in the following insolvency procedures.[157] As a consequence, Andrea Francovich and the other claimants brought action against the State of Italy in an attempt to obtain their unsettled wages by course of law, establishing their claim on guarantees provided for by Directive 80/987.[158] They were pleading the judges either to order the defendant to settle their outstanding wages, exercising the rights conferred upon them by the directive, or to hold it accountable for the sustained loss arising from the incorrect transposition of the directive into national law.[159]

In light of matters pertaining to Community law, two district courts in Italy brought the matter before the ECJ under Art. 177 EEC [*ex Art. 234 TEC; now Art. 267 TFEU*].[160] The preliminary ruling requests were initiated by first instance judges from the Magistrate's Courts of the Italian cities of Bassano del Grappa and Vicenza who adjudicated issues pertaining to industrial relations and in principle to litigation by employees.[161] In the course of the proceedings the two district judges had chosen to refer particular questions to the Court, which interestingly were formulated in the same way in both causes, most likely because the same attorney advised the claimants in the two cases.[162] The first question brought up two matters that the ECJ scrutinized individually. The first matter was whether or not the directive gave rise to rights that had direct effect.

155 Cf. Bebr, 1992, pp. 558-559.
156 Cf. *Francovich* (fn 1), paras 5-6.
157 Cf. Caranta, 1993, p. 277.
158 Cf. Hanft, 1991, p. 1259.
159 Cf. Caranta, 1993, p. 277.
160 Cf. Hanft, 1991, p. 1259.
161 Cf. Caranta, 1993, p. 277.
162 Cf. ibid, pp. 277-278

The second matter was whether or not the Member State was legally responsible for loss and damage due to infringement of Community law. The remaining two questions, which had been referred, were related to the guarantees pertaining to the restitution of wages that the Member State had to make available in case that the directive gave rise to individual rights.[163]

3.2 Judgment of the Court

Notably, the Court, as was pointed out by Bebr, was asked by the Italian Government to declare the judgment in plenary sitting with all judges present, which highlighted the great significance of the case.[164] In its judgment, it held the Italian State responsible for the damages sustained by the claimants due to non-implementation of the Directive 80/987 within the required time limit for transposition.

3.2.1 Direct Effect of the Directive

Regarding the question of direct effect of the directive, the Court decided that the directive did not confer rights upon individuals on which they could directly depend. It substantiated this decision by revisiting its previous judgment in *Becker*,[165] in which it had laid down the specific requirements for a directive to have direct effect. The ECJ held that

> wherever the provisions of a directive appear (...) to be unconditional and sufficiently precise, those provisions may, in the absence of implementing measures adopted within the prescribed period, be relied upon as against any national provision which is incompatible with the directive or in so far as the provisions of the directive define rights which individuals are able to assert against the [Member] State.[166]

Consequently, the Court assessed these criteria by scrutinizing what the substance of the directive in question was and who the respective parties, such as the beneficiaries and the guarantor were.[167] It established that the provisions of the directive defined the beneficiaries and that, by laying down a minimum guarantee, they were unconditional as well as sufficiently precise when it came to the substance of the guarantee. Nonetheless, the ECJ observed that they did

---

163 Cf. Hanft, 1991, p. 1259.
164 Cf. Bebr, 1992, p. 566.
165 *Becker* (fn 60).
166 Ibid, para 25.
167 Cf. Hanft, 1991, p. 1260.

not explicitly define the guarantor.[168] According to the provisions of Directive 80/987, it was incumbent upon the Member States to determine the party authoritative for the guarantees it established. Thus, the national authorities might have obliged a private organization, such as, for instance, a collective insurance company managed by trade unions.[169] However, it made clear that the obligations of the Member States conferred by the directive to fund such a system of paying unsettled claims by employees as a whole did not extend as far as to entail that a Member State could be particularly qualified as the party establishing the guarantee as laid down by the directive. Therefore, the obligation to pay unsettled claims was only up to the defined guarantee institution and not to the Member State.[170] Against this background, the Court went on to declare that in the case where the Member State did not comply with its obligation to transpose the directive within the required time limit, it could not be deduced from the wording of the directive nor from the facts that the Member State had to be regarded as the guarantor. Finally, applying the norm it had established in *Becker*, the ECJ decided that the directive in this case did not have direct effect.[171]

3.2.2 Liability of the State for Breaches of Community Law

Having addressed the first part of the first question, the Court in turn focused on the second part of the question. It expressed the second part of the question in different words to examine the obligation of the State of Italy to recover the damages of the claimants, which they had sustained due to the omission of the State in transposing the directive in good time. The ECJ expanded the question by taking into account the liability of Member States for damages resulting out of breaches of Community law.[172] In particular the Court scrutinized both the availability and the restrictions of liability pertaining to non-transposition or incorrect transposition of Community law bringing about damage and loss to individuals.[173]

In this course it observed that the liability for damages caused by a breach of obligations under Community law emanated from both the general system of the Treaty and Art. 5 EEC [*ex Art. 10 TEC; now Art. 4(3) TEU*].[174] The ECJ built upon the foundations it had laid down in *Van Gend en Loos*[175] reprising that the Community established a new legal order for which the Member States have

168 Cf. ibid, pp. 1260-1261.
169 Cf. Caranta, 1993, p. 278.
170 Cf. Bebr, 1992, p. 567.
171 Cf. Hanft, 1991, p. 1261.
172 Cf. ibid.
173 Cf. Caranta, 1993, p. 278.
174 Cf. Hanft, 1991, pp. 1261-1262.
175 *Van Gend en Loos* (fn 5).

restricted the exercise of their sovereign powers,[176] and that "Community law (...) not only imposes obligations on individuals but is also intended to confer upon them rights which become part of their legal heritage".[177] The Court also made a reference to its previous jurisprudence, in particular *Amministrazione delle Finanze dello Stato v. Simmenthal SpA*,[178] and *Factortame I*,[179] which laid down the principle of effective protection of rights under Community law, a doctrine authoritative of introducing new duties and conveying new jurisdiction upon the national courts of the Member States. Revisiting its most important jurisprudence, the ECJ consequently held it to be irreconcilable with the effectiveness both of Community law and of judicial protection to dismiss a claim against the State by private parties who had sustained damage because of a violation of Community law. This was especially appropriate in circumstances such as those in the present case, where the laws did not create direct effect.[180] Finally, the Court placed reliance on Art. 5 EEC, which bound Member States to adopt appropriate measures to make sure that their obligations under Community law were fulfilled,[181] one in particular by virtue of the ECJ was "to make good loss and damage caused to individuals by breaches of Community law for which they can be held responsible".[182]

3.2.3 Conditions for State Liability Under Francovich

After having determined the rule under which Member States had to recover damages inflicted by their violation of Community law, the Court in *Francovich* laid the focus on the requirements under which State liability might be established.[183] It proceeded to state that the requirements for a right to damages to be established under the Treaties relied on the type of infringement of Community law that was at stake.[184] Consequently, if the act or rule of Community law could be deemed as relevant for the concerns of private parties, if it could be qualified accordingly in the specific legal source or instrument, and if a sufficient causal relationship could be justified between the damage of the claimant and the omission of the State, then a tenable claim for recovery of damages emerged.[185]

---

176 Cf. Hanft, 1991, p. 1261.
177 *Van Gend en Loos* (fn 5), para 12.
178 Case 106/77 *Amministrazione delle Finanze dello Stato v. Simmenthal SpA (Simmenthal II)* [1978] ECR 629.
179 *Factortame I* (fn 135).
180 Cf. Caranta, 1993, pp. 278-279.
181 Cf. Hanft, 1991, pp. 1261-1262.
182 *Francovich* (fn 1), para 37.
183 Cf. Caranta, 1993, p. 283.
184 Cf. Hanft, 1991, p. 1262.
185 Cf. Ross, 1993, p. 62.

In *Francovich* the ECJ held in particular that when three requirements were fulfilled, then individuals had a right to recovery of damages in case a Member State was in default of its obligation under Art. 189(3) EEC [*ex Art. 249(3) TEC; now Art. 288(3) TFEU*].[186] The requirements determined by the Court were the following:

> The first of those conditions is that the result prescribed by the directive should entail the *grant of rights to individuals*.
>
> The second condition is that it should be possible to *identify the content of those rights* on the basis of the provisions of the directive.
>
> Finally, the third condition is the *existence of a causal link* between the breach of the State's obligation and the loss and damage suffered by the injured parties.[187]

It was these requirements, as had been observed by the ECJ, which were both essential and sufficient for the right to liability to emerge. According to Caranta, the principle of State liability for violations of Community law laid down in *Francovich* had to be characterized as a system of strict liability, where fault was deemed to be not important. Consequently, the burden of proof lay on behalf of the State as a defendant.[188]

Out of the three requirements, the third, entailing the occurrence of both damage and a causal connection, was undoubtedly beyond question. The other two requirements warranted a closer analysis: with regard to the second requirement, that was the task of scrutinizing the subject matter of the right afforded to individuals under provision of Community law impinged, it could be established that the Court was no more stringent than in the theory where the direct effect of directives was under consideration. As a matter of fact, the conferment of rights by the directive had already been set up in the present case. It was the direct effect of its provisions, which had been exempted, because the bearer, and not the beneficiary, of the respective obligation could not be distinctly ascertained on the basis of the rules of the directive. For this purpose, the ECJ employed, in the particular issue of whether a conferment of rights could be es-

186 Cf. Hanft, 1991, p. 1262.
187 *Francovich* (fn 1), para 40 (emphasis added).
188 Cf. Caranta, 1993, p. 283.

tablished, the basis of the guidelines,[189] which had been developed in the well-established case law in *Van Gend en Loos*.[190]

A pivotal aspect in the precise demarcation of the boundaries of the recently developed type of State liability by the Court in *Francovich* lay in the first requirement laid down in the judgment, namely that the rule breached was intended to afford an individual with legal protection by conferring upon him a particular right.[191] In the view held by Caranta, this criterion was partly influenced by a prerequisite evolved by the jurisprudence of the ECJ pertaining to the non-contractual liability of the Community institutions under Art. 215(2) EEC [*ex Art. 288(2) TEC; now Art. 340(2) TFEU*].[192] Under the non-contractual liability of the Community, there was the requirement, laid down in the so-called *Schöppenstedt*[193] formula, that the rule of Community law breached had to be a "superior rule of law for the protection of the individual"[194]. Consequently, under the jurisprudence of the Court, this requirement had been construed so loosely that it was met if the provisions impinged were considered to safeguard both individual and general interests.[195] In his opinion in the case, AG Mischo suggested basing the requirements of the *Francovich* principle of State liability on the conditions of non-contractual liability of the Community.[196] However, the ECJ did not heed the opinion of the Advocate General. Instead, it endorsed part of the conjecture, which entailed "that the provision violated by the act should have been introduced with the aim of protecting an individual"[197], and held that the existence of a sufficiently serious breach of a superior rule was not necessary, any infringement of a rule of Community law was ascertained to be sufficient to incur liability of the State. In this context, Caranta put forward that the lack of any referral to the superior character of the provision was barely remarkable, as the legal order of the Community was of itself and in principle higher-ranking to domestic law, but the taciturnity of the Court on the 'seriousness' of the infringement spoke volumes.[198] In the light of this a divergence between the State liability and liability of the Community could be established. Whereas for the latter a sufficiently serious breach was required, no such criterion was deemed to be necessary for the *Francovich* principle. As a consequence, it could be de-

[189] See, to that effect, chapter 2.1.4 Direct Effect of Community Law, p. 10.
[190] Cf. Caranta, 1993, p. 283.
[191] Cf. ibid.
[192] Cf. ibid, p. 284.
[193] Case 5/71 *Zuckerfabrik Schöppenstedt v. Council (Schöppenstedt)* [1971] ECR 975.
[194] Ibid, para 11.
[195] Cf. Gutman, 2011, p. 713.
[196] Cf. Opinion of AG Mischo in *Francovich* (fn 89), paras 71 et seqq.
[197] Caranta, 1993, p. 284.
[198] Cf. ibid.

duced from the case that the ECJ was stricter to Member States than to institutions of the Community.[199]

Thus, in the event of fulfillment of these three requirements, the Court stipulated that reparation had to be provided for an infringement of Community law in the same scope as it would be provided for an equivalent claim against a Member State under domestic law.[200]

However, different from the substantive rules for the liability of the Member States, which were laid down by Community law, the procedural rules for the right to claim damages were according to the particular domestic law of a Member State.[201] Consequently, the ECJ determined that, in the absence of legal harmonization within the Community, it was up to "the internal legal order of each Member State to designate the competent courts and lay down the detailed procedural rules for legal proceedings intended fully to safeguard the rights which individuals derive from Community law".[202] By so ruling, Court sought to overcome the procedural hurdle of the liability and pointed to its previous jurisprudence, particularly to *Rewe*[203] and *Russo*,[204] where it made clear that it was left to the respective national legal systems of the Member States to guarantee the effectiveness of Community rules and to safeguard the rights that they conveyed to private parties. As the judgment rested on the first question that had been referred to the ECJ, it deemed that it was not required to answer the other two remaining questions.[205]

3.3 Concluding Observations

The ruling in *Francovich* was just the first advance in expanding the non-contractual liability of the Member States.[206] In the case, the Court examined the rights and reliefs that were available to individuals in the event that an unimplemented directive did not have direct effect. In its assessment it came to the conclusion that, despite lacking transposition, the directive conveyed a recognizable right upon individuals for which recovery of damages could be an effective legal relief.[207]

199 Cf. ibid, pp. 284-285.
200 Cf. Hanft, 1991, p. 1262.
201 Cf. Bebr, 1992, p. 570.
202 *Francovich* (fn 1), para 42.
203 *Rewe* (fn 115).
204 *Russo* (fn 96).
205 Cf. Hanft, 1991, p. 1263.
206 Cf. Bebr, 1992, p. 583.
207 Cf. Hanft, 1991, p. 1257.

The Court, on one side, acknowledged the principle of State liability under Community law in relatively broad terms. On the other side, it made it explicit that the mere presence of the right to reparation would not be enough to enjoy it. To this end, the ECJ held that established criteria had to be fulfilled. What the criteria were, under which a right to compensation existed, relied upon "the nature of the breach"[208]. However, in the ruling, the Court only laid down the criteria to be met in the event of a default of a Member State in adopting a directive in accordance with Art. 189(3) EEC, specifically in the case of non-implementation of a directive.[209]

The most significant element was that in *Francovich*, the plaintiffs could not benefit from the principle of direct effect.[210] As a consequence, the ECJ, in its judgment, took into account the necessity of filling the lacuna in legal protection comprised by direct and indirect effect. Thus, it could be held that the seminal ruling of the Court reduced to some degree the absence of horizontal effect concerning directives. The ruling took away any ambition of the Member States to not transpose a directive in a timely manner and it afforded relief, if requirements for State liability were met, for individuals to bring legal action against the State such as in cases when directives had no direct effect, but conferred rights upon individuals.[211] For the convenience of the reader, the main aspects of the judgment are illustrated in Figure 2.[212]

Still, in spite of the significance of the principle of State liability, the ruling in *Francovich* provided very little guidelines for the cases to come.[213] Ross even opined that the judgment of the ECJ was "typically paradoxical",[214] and blended "terseness of expression with expansiveness of principle"[215] creating a plethora of controversies and complications as a result.[216] For instance, it was not resolved to which degree the *Francovich* principle was applicable in other cases that did not involve a non-implementation of a directive and what the exact stipulations would be pertaining to the other types of infringements of Community law.[217] Furthermore, the judgment did not elucidate whether the principle was applicable in cases of rights with direct effect, or whether it was a legal relief of final instance where all other remedies had been exhausted, or a substantive

208 *Francovich* (fn 1), para 38.
209 Cf. Prechal, 2006, pp. 276-277.
210 Cf. ibid.
211 Cf. Kent, 2008, p. 111.
212 See Figure 2: The Francovich Judgment at a Glance, p. 36.
213 Cf. Craig & de Búrca, 2011, p. 243.
214 Ross, 1993, p. 58.
215 Ibid.
216 Cf. ibid.
217 Cf. Prechal, 2006, p. 277.

and absolute right.[218] Moreover, some questions arose on the extent of the infringement necessary to incur liability of the State, namely if it was required that it would have to be grave and manifest, and whether there was a prerequisite of fault to be established. Other questions dealt with the availability of the *Francovich* remedy concerning class action, whether Member States could require that an infringement proceeding, or a proceeding for failure to act had to be initiated first in regards to any national act contrary to Community law, before granting recovery of damages, for which heads of damage reparation had to be afforded, how to measure the amount of damage, and what the point in time was from which the responsibility to make reparation came into existence.[219]

As a consequence, it did not come unexpected that further explanation and development was anticipated.[220] However, regarding these issues, Harlow pointed out that "for several years after *Francovich* there was a golden silence".[221] Indeed, despite the Court affirming the *Francovich* principle in the following judgments of *Faccini Dori,*[222] *Wagner Miret,*[223] and *El Corte Inglés SA v. Rivero*[224],[225] it was not until 1996, when the ECJ would finally have the opportunity to address several of these unresolved issues in the case of *Brasserie du Pêcheur/Factortame III*[226].[227]

---

218 Cf. Ross, 1993, p. 58.
219 Cf. Wooldridge & D'Sa, 1996, pp. 161-162.
220 Cf. Bebr, 1992, p. 583.
221 Harlow, 1996, p. 202.
222 Case C-91/92 *Paola Faccini Dori v. Recreb Srl (Faccini Dori)* [1994] ECR I-3325.
223 Case C-334/92 *Teodoro Wagner Miret v. Fondo de Garantía Salarial (Wagner Miret)* [1993] ECR I-6911.
224 Case C-192/94 *El Corte Inglés SA v. Cristina Blázquez Rivero (El Corte Inglés)* [1996] ECR I-1281.
225 Cf. Kent, 2008, p. 111.
226 *Brasserie/Factortame III* (fn 11).
227 Cf. Prechal, 2006, p. 277.

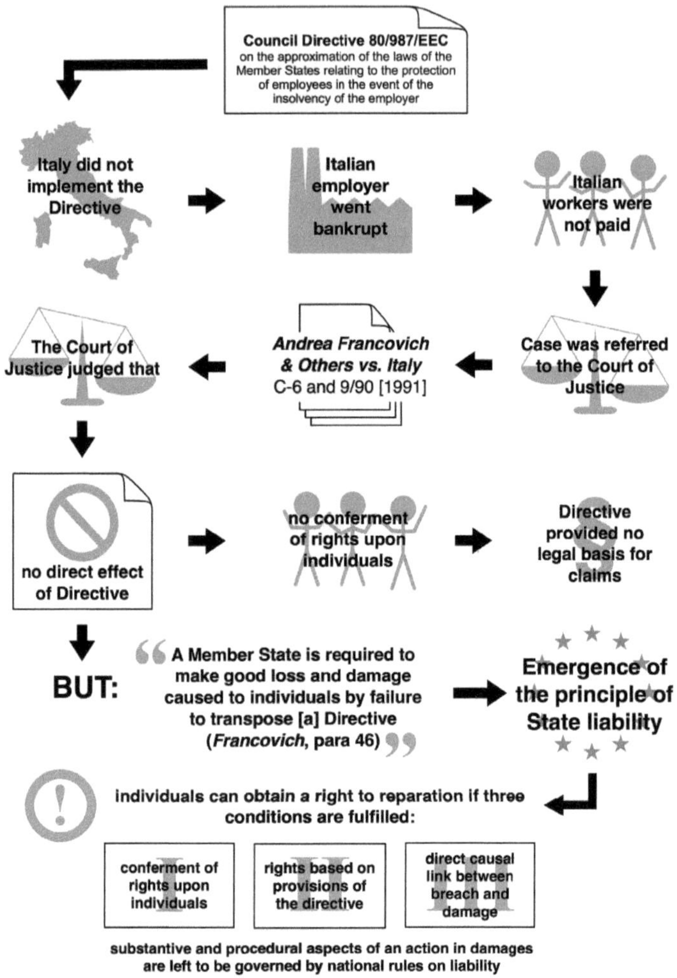

Figure 2: The Francovich Judgment at a Glance

Figure 2. The main aspects of the judgment in *Francovich* which established the principle of Member State Liability in damages in the legal order of the Community. In *Francovich* the point of departure was the failure of Italy to transpose into national laws a directive that protected employees in case their employers went bankrupt. The claimants, who were owed arrears of pay from their insolvent employer, brought action against the State of Italy in an attempt to obtain their unsettled payments. The Italian courts, unsure of how to decide the case, referred to the ECJ for a preliminary ruling. The Court of Justice observed that although the directive was not directly effective, thus conferring no rights upon individuals which they could rely on before national courts, it was the duty of a Member State to afford reparation to individuals in the event of non-implementation of a directive. The European Court held that individuals could obtain a right to reparation under EC law if three conditions were fulfilled.

Source: Own compilation.

4 Conditions for Implementing State Liability: Brasserie du Pêcheur / Factortame III

4.1 Factual and Procedural Background

In *Commission v. Germany*,[228] also known as the *Beer Purity* case, Germany was found to be in breach of Art. 30 EEC [*ex Art. 28 TEC; now Art. 34 TFEU*], because German legislation prohibited the import of beer which failed to meet the *Reinheitsgebot* (Purity Requirement) pursuant to Arts. 9 and 10 *Biersteuergesetz* (German Beer Taxation Act).[229] According to this act it was forbidden to place on the market in Germany any beverage described as *Bier* if it consisted of ingredients other than water, hops, malt and yeast. Although in the wake of the judgment, the national provision conflicting with the free movement of goods in the Community was promptly revised, up to that point beer producers in the Member States had been excluded from exporting their product to the German market.[230]

Consequently, a French brewery situated in Alsace with the name of Brasserie du Pêcheur SA filed a claim for damages against the German State for the loss sustained from 1981 to 1987 due to the import limitation in that period. The company sought reparation of DM1.8 million,[231] which, according to it, was only a small fraction of the actual incurred loss. Both German district courts *Landgericht* and *Oberlandesgericht* rejected the claim and Brasserie du Pêcheur SA filed an appeal to the *Bundesgerichtshof* (German Federal Court of Justice).[232]

At the time German national law only established non-contractual State liability for injury or loss incurred to a natural or legal person, but only in the event when there was a violation of authoritative obligations conferred upon the German State as against a third party (*Drittbezogenheit*),[233] or illegitimate intervention similar to dispossession. The *Bundesgerichtshof* observed that neither case was applicable. The German Beer Taxation Act had not been directed at individuals, there were no other addressees that would give rise to State liability, nor in regard to illegitimate intervention could loss, emerging from a provision that was unconstitutional, derive the right to damages. As a consequence, ac-

228 Case 178/84, *Commission v. Germany (Beer Purity)* [1987] ECR 1227.
229 Cf. ibid, para 54; cf. Arts. 9-10 German Beer Taxation Act (Biersteuergesetz/BStG) of 14. March 1952, BGBl. I, p. 149.
230 Cf. Convery, 1997, p. 605.
231 Approximately €1.3 million (adjusted for inflation).
232 Cf. Puder, 2000, p. 317.
233 Cf. Art. 839(1) German Civil Code (Bürgerliches Gesetzbuch/BGB) *icw.* Art. 34 German Constitution (Grundgesetz/GG).

cording to German law, Brasserie du Pêcheur SA was left without legal relief. However, the *Bundesgerichtshof* brought up and referred multiple questions to the Court as to whether or not it was permissible and warranted to establish such a legal relief based upon appropriate rules of Community law.[234]

The case of Brasserie du Pêcheur SA was combined with the British case of Factortame Ltd, the third installment of a succession of legal disputes pertaining to a new registration system of fishing boats in the United Kingdom under the Merchant Shipping Act 1988.[235] These disputes emerged from rules restraining, on the basis of nationality and residence, the likelihood of maintaining, managing and crewing fishing vessels under the British flag.[236] In *Factortame I*,[237] the ECJ decided that the exemption of the Crown from interim relief, precluding the application of a rule, could not be unconditional, and such a rule in cases where it was not compatible with Community law must be disapplied. In *Factortame II*,[238] the Court held that specific limitations on the grounds of nationality that were part of the Merchant Shipping Act 1988 were contradictory to Community law. It followed that Factortame Ltd and several other similar claimants who had been precluded from such registration subsequently would desire, apart from declaratory and interim relief, reparation for the damages sustained as consequence of being denied the right to fish. This desire was the point of departure of *Brasserie/Factortame III*[239].[240]

However, on that point several difficulties emerged, because under English law no principle of reparation for losses sustained by reason of legislation, similar to the *Francovich*[241] doctrine, was in existence. On the contrary, public authorities were accountable under the common principles of liability under civil law. Thus, infringements of Community law could be regarded either as breach of statutory duty or as misfeasance.[242] In that context, a decisive case in English law for State liability was the ruling of the Court of Appeal in *Bourgoin*[243].

In *Bourgoin*, the English court held that, under national law, a claimant must base its application for remedy in damages upon a recognized reason of action in tort. The matter was appealed and came before the House of Lords which

234 Cf. Lane, 1996, p. 94.
235 Cf. Lee, 2000, p. 10.
236 Cf. Caranta, 2008, p. 202.
237 *Factortame I* (fn 135).
238 Case C-221/89 *The Queen v. Secretary of State for Transport, ex parte Factortame Ltd & Others (Factortame II)* [1991] ECR I-3905.
239 *Brasserie/Factortame III* (fn 11).
240 Cf. Lee, 2000, p. 10.
241 *Francovich* (fn 1).
242 Cf. Harlow & Rawlings, 2010, p. 775.
243 *Bourgoin v. Minister for Agriculture, Fisheries and Food* [1985] 3 All ER 585.

held in majority that Art. 30 EEC (and likewise Art. 52 EEC [*ex Art. 43 TEC; now Art. 49 TFEU*]) only afforded public law rights to subjects under the law. The implication being that it gave standing to dispute the legitimacy of an act of a public authority for an imputable breach only by the way of judicial review, and therefore courts would be able to adjudicate damages only in case of the exclusively public law tort of misfeasance in public office.[244] However, the extent of this tort was to some degree restrained because it was required to demonstrate malice or actual awareness of the wrongful act.[245]

Since misfeasance could not be attributed to the English Parliament, the claims put forward by Factortame Ltd and the other plaintiffs, according to English law, were to fail. The remaining question was whether legal relief was afforded under Community law. Therefore, the High Court of England, as the *Bundesgerichtshof*, referred the subject to the ECJ for a preliminary ruling.[246]

The joined cases of *Brasserie du Pêcheur* and *Factortame III* have several facts in common.[247] Firstly, they both involved violations of the Treaty. In contrast to *Francovich*, neither case concerned the implementation of a directive, but rather dealt with acts of the State that were conflicting with provisions of primary law of the Community.[248] Moreover, the Court had long-since established that these provisions had direct effect.[249] Secondly, both violations were caused through a failure at legislative level.[250] On the one hand, for Brasserie du Pêcheur SA, the harm was inflicted by the inaction of the legislative body to annul or revise an existing provision that was conflicting with Community law, on the other hand Factortame Ltd faced a legal act which introduced a clause of a provision that infringed upon the Community rights of individuals.[251] Thirdly, the actions brought by both claimants before the national courts were dismissed.[252] In none of these cases was there a possibility of trying to obtain restitution under the applicable national laws.[253]

Furthermore, the damage in both cases was one of economic loss, which according to rules of private in law in both Member States Germany and England would not establish a right to recovery of damages, because there was no duty

244 Cf. Lane, 1996, pp. 95-96.
245 Cf. Van Gerven, 1996, p. 511.
246 Cf. Lane, 1996, pp. 95-96.
247 Cf. ibid, p. 96.
248 Cf. Lee, 2000, p. 10.
249 Cf. *Brasserie/Factortame III* (fn 11), para 23.
250 Cf. Lane, 1996, p. 96.
251 Cf. Biondi & Farley, 2009, p. 21.
252 Cf. Lane, 1996, p. 96.
253 Cf. Biondi & Farley, 2009, p. 21.

of care. Consequently, this issue brought up two difficulties. First, the issue clearly demonstrated that the reliance on domestic rules and procedures of the Member States would give rise to legal remedies pertaining to damages being different in every Member State. This was in contrast to the legal order of the Community which postulated the application of Community law and the making available of Community rights in an uniform manner. Second, most rights emanating from the Treaties were economic rights. If Member States could adhere to a principle in their national legal systems that there was no duty of care pertaining to public non-contractual liability in case of pure economic loss, any remedial action in damages for violation of Community rights would be severely constrained.[254]

As a consequence, the crucial issues, which the ECJ had to consider in its preliminary ruling, were, firstly whether the principle of State liability established in *Francovich* was applicable to acts of the national legislature, secondly, what the requirements were for such a right to reparation under Community law, thirdly, whether this right to damages could be made subject to the existence of fault, fourthly the rules on determining the quantum of damages, and lastly, the amount of time considered by the reparation.[255]

4.2 Judgment of the Court

4.2.1 Revisiting the Principle of State Liability

At the outset, the Court called to mind its ruling in *Francovich* implying that Member States were required to redress any harm inflicted on individuals resulting from violations of Community law for which they could be held liable.[256] It then cast aside two alleged restrictions to the development of the principle of Member State liability.[257]

According to the reasoning of the German, Dutch, and Irish governments, an action in damages was to be considered as only a subsidiary remedial action, to correct a lacuna and to be obtainable only in circumstances where there was no other way of putting into effect a Community right. This line of reasoning stemmed from *Francovich* in which the ECJ held the directive at issue to be not directly effective.[258]

254 Cf. Lane, 1996, p. 97.
255 Cf. Puder, 2000, p. 318.
256 Cf. *Brasserie/Factortame III* (fn 11), para 17; cf. *Francovich* (fn 1), para 37.
257 Cf. Puder, 2000, p. 319.
258 Cf. *Francovich* (fn 1), para 26; cf. Lane, 1996, p. 97.

The Court made short work of this first allegation. Referring to its own long-standing case law, [259] it observed that the principle of direct effect was not adequate on its own to guarantee the full and complete transposition of a directive. Specifically, the principle could not avert harm being inflicted upon individuals flowing from the default of a Member State in implementing the directive. In the event of a person sustaining damages by virtue of an infringement of a rule with direct effect, the right to reparation was the "necessary corollary"[260] of that directly effective rule.[261] Thus, it followed that the two remedies were not precluding each other.[262]

Then, the ECJ addressed the contention of Germany that only legislative bodies could inflict liability in damages and that, by interfering in these affairs, the Court had actually taken lawmaking authority itself.[263] Dealing with the second allegation, it pronounced that its jurisdiction to assess inquiries pertaining to Community law involved adjudicating "the existence and extent of State liability for damage ensuing as a result of a breach of obligations incumbent on the State by virtue of Community law"[264]. The ECJ deduced that both its principal duty and the authority of interpretation were enshrined in the primary law of the Community requiring it to make certain that "in the interpretation and application of the Treaty the law is observed"[265]. This duty, it went on making reference to Art. 164 EEC [*ex Art. 220(1) TEC; now Art. 19(1) TEU*], covered judging on an inquiry according to common practices of interpretation, especially referring to the fundamental principles of Community law and, where required, to principles of law common to the national legal orders of the Member States.[266]

The Court expanded on this point of departure by connecting the State liability rules to the principle of non-contractual liability of the Community under Art. 215 EEC [*ex Art. 288 TEC; now Art. 340 TFEU*], in turn describing it as "simply an expression of the general principle familiar to the legal systems of the Member States that an unlawful act or omission gives rise to an obligation to make good the damage caused"[267].[268]

---

259 Cf. Case C-119/89 *Commission v. Spain (Spanish VAT Importation)* [1991] ECR I-641, para 9; cf. Case C-120/88 *Commission v. Italy (Italian VAT Importation)* [1991] ECR I-621, para 10; cf. Case 168/85 *Commission v. Italy (Access to Professions)* [1986] ECR 2945, para 11.

260 *Brasserie/Factortame III* (fn 11), para 22.

261 Cf. Oliver, 1997, p. 642.

262 Cf. Lane, 1996, p. 97.

263 Cf. Oliver, 1997, p. 642.

264 *Brasserie/Factortame III* (fn 11), para 25.

265 Ibid, para 27.

266 Cf. Puder, 2000, pp. 320-321.

267 *Brasserie/Factortame III* (fn 11), para 29.

Then, the ECJ answered the question, which had been raised by both courts making the preliminary reference, as to whether Member States were obliged to make reparation for wrongful actions or failures arising from its legislators.[269] On that point, it made clear that State liability in damages may be established not just in cases where Member States, but also where domestic law making bodies by positive action were in breach of Community law. The Court went on to state that the liability in damages of Member States was a universal principle. Since it was "inherent in the system of the Treaty", [270] it held "good for any case in which a Member State breaches Community law, whatever be the organ of the State whose act or omission was responsible for the breach"[271]. As a result, it could be deduced that a Member State was accountable regardless of which State authority occasioned the damage.[272]

Against the background, the ECJ referred to its judgment in *Zuckerfabriken*[273] where it held that "[the] uniform application [of Community law] is a fundamental requirement of the Community legal order", [274] therefore, keeping with long-standing case law,[275] the obtainability of State liability "cannot depend on domestic rules [on] the division of powers between [state] authorities"[276]. In conclusion, it put emphasis on this argument by pronouncing that this rule flowed from public international law and it must *a fortiori* be applicable in the legal system of the Community.[277]

4.2.2 Conditions for Incurring Liability

The Court addressed the circumstances under which Member States would be responsible for wrongful acts or omissions of their legislature. First it emphasized that State liability in damages was fundamentally existent in the system of the Treaties. As previously laid down in *Francovich*, the principle of State liability was conditional upon the type of breach, and additionally had to take into consideration the general principles of Community law such as the judicial protection of individual rights, the full effectiveness and uniform application of Community law and the duty of loyal cooperation. For the purpose of determin-

---

268 Cf. Betlem, 1996, (*A. The Ius Commune Regime* section, para 4).
269 Cf. Oliver, 1997, p. 643.
270 *Brasserie/Factortame III* (fn 11), para 31.
271 Ibid, para 32.
272 Cf. Tridimas, 1996, p. 412.
273 Joined Cases C-143/88 and C-92/89 *Zuckerfabrik Süderdithmarschen AG v. Hauptzollamt Itzehoe and Zuckerfabrik Soest GmbH v. Hauptzollamt Paderborn (Zuckerfabriken)* [1991] ECR I-415.
274 Ibid, para 26.
275 Cf. Case 77/69 *Commission v. Belgium* [1970] ECR 237, para 15.
276 *Brasserie/Factortame III* (fn 11), para 33.
277 Cf. Puder, 2000, p. 319.

ing suitable conditions, it was appropriate to make reference to the jurisprudence of the ECJ on non-contractual liability on behalf of the Community.[278]

At this juncture it shall be noted that this was not totally unexpected. Harmonization of the conditions of State liability and non-contractual liability of the Community had for some time been an issue wished for by Advocates Generals Mischo,[279] van Gerven,[280] and Tesauro[281]. The only Advocate General, who remained skeptical,[282] was AG Léger.[283] However, the Court took a more positive stance on the utilization of the conditions of the principle of non-contractual liability of the Community to serve for the purposes of State liability than put forward by AG Léger. It maintained that it was important to touch upon this jurisprudence, because the safeguarding of rights that Community law conferred upon individuals could not be different in nature depending on whether a national State authority or an institution of the Community occasioned the damage.[284]

The connection between the *Francovich* doctrine and the non-contractual liability regime under Art. 215 EEC was very useful in substantiating the viewpoint that an infringement of Community law by domestic legislative bodies could establish liability on behalf of the Member State, because the obligation under the article additionally dealt with the responsibility of the Community for wrongful behavior of its law making institutions. It also permitted the ECJ to deploy the same "strict approach",[285] which it had established earlier under the *Schöppenstedt* formula,[286] adapted toward the liability of the legislative institutions of the Community to the liability of legislature of the Member States.[287] In *Schöppenstedt*, the Court notably held that, when it came to legislative activities that comprised "measures of economic policy",[288] liability was not incurred by the Community except when a "sufficiently flagrant violation of a superior rule of law for the protection of the individual [has] occurred"[289]. Whereas the reference to

278 Cf. Lane, 1996, p. 97.
279 Cf. Opinion of AG Mischo in *Francovich* (fn 89), paras 71 et seqq.
280 Cf. Opinion of AG Van Gerven in Case C-128/92 *Banks v. British Coal* [1994] ECR I-1209, paras 49 et seqq.
281 Cf. Opinion of AG Tesauro in Joined Cases C-46/93 and C-48/93 *Brasserie du Pêcheur SA v. Germany and The Queen v. Secretary of State for Transport, ex parte Factortame Ltd & Others* [1996] ECR I-1029, paras 61 et seqq.
282 Cf. Opinion of AG Léger in Case C-5/94 *The Queen v. Ministry of Agriculture, Fisheries and Food, ex parte Hedley Lomas* [1996] ECR I-2553, paras 138 et seqq.
283 Cf. Lane, 1996, p. 98.
284 Cf. *Brasserie/Factortame III* (fn 11), para 42; cf. Wooldridge & D'Sa, 1996, p. 163.
285 *Brasserie/Factortame III* (fn 11), para 45.
286 *Schöppenstedt* (fn 193).
287 Cf. Van Gerven, 1996, p. 519.
288 *Schöppenstedt* (fn 193), para 11.
289 Ibid.

economic policy, made by the ECJ, was purely exemplary and thus had to be considered in a broad sense as was illustrated by its subsequent jurisprudence[290].[291]

In *Bayerische HNL*,[292] a significant case that followed, the Court refined the language of the criteria for liability of the Community. It introduced the wording "sufficiently serious breach"[293] and established that where the legislature had wide discretion in exercise of its legislative function, then the liability of the Community would only be established in cases where an institution had "manifestly and gravely disregarded the limits on the exercise of its powers"[294].[295] Notably, the reference to *Schöppenstedt* unavoidably paved the way for the coherent evolution of the law: if non-contractual liability of the Community was able to have an impact on the liability of the State, then the opposite must also hold valid. In fact, in the latter judgment of *Bergaderm v. Commission*[296] the ECJ turned the association the other way by firstly referring to its jurisprudence on State liability to lay down the criteria to be applied for the non-contractual liability of the Community[297].[298]

Moreover, the Court determined that the reasoning in this jurisprudence, that is to say the necessity to steer clear of excessively constraining the legislative functions of the institutions of the Community, was equally binding for the national legislative authorities of the Member States. Nonetheless, it was quick in drawing attention to the fact that Member States, in their exercise of powers in the scope of Community law, were not always afforded with a wide discretion.[299]

Subsequently, the ECJ scrutinized whether or not in the cases of *Brasserie* and *Factortame III* the respective Member States enjoyed a wide discretion in the

---

290 See, e.g. Case C-63/89 *Assurances du Credit v. Council and Commission* [1991] ECR I-1799.

291 Cf. Hilson, 2005, p. 678.

292 Joined Cases 83/76 and 94/76, 4/77, 15/77 and 40/77 *Bayerische HNL Vermehrungsbetriebe GmbH & Co. KG & Others v. Council and Commission of the European Communities (Bayerische HNL)* [1978] ECR 1209.

293 Ibid, para 4.

294 Ibid, para 6.

295 Cf. Hilson, 2005, p. 679.

296 Case C-352/98 P *Laboratoires Pharmaceutiques Bergaderm and Goupil v. Commission (Bergaderm)* [2000] ECR I-5291.

297 For the purposes of this paper, non-contractual liability of the Union shall not be examined in detail; see, to that effect, Gutman, K. (2011). The evolution of the action for damages against the European Union and its place in the system of judicial protection. *Common Market Law Review, 48*, 695–750; see also Hilson, C. (2005). The role of discretion in EC law on non-contractual liability. *Common Market Law Review, 42*, 677–695.

298 Cf. Tridimas, 2001, p. 322.

299 Cf. Oliver, 1997, p. 644.

exercise of their powers. Setting apart the case of *Francovich*, in which the Member State was under a well-defined duty to attain a specific outcome, from those of *Brasserie* and *Factortame III*, the Court recognized that in the latter cases the Member States were endowed with a wide discretion. In such cases, where circumstances implied making choices when implementing legislative acts, it ruled that the following three requirements must be met to establish a right to damages under the legal order of the Community:[300]

> [Firstly,] the rule of law infringed must be intended to confer rights on individuals; [secondly,] the breach must be sufficiently serious; [thirdly,] there must be a direct causal link between the breach of the obligation resting on the State and the damage sustained by the injured parties.[301]

As these requirements, in principle, were reiterations of two of the three conditions laid down in *Francovich*, neither of them came as a bolt from the blue. However, it was the second requirement, which was novel and had crucial meaning.[302] It resulted from the jurisprudence of the ECJ in regard to the non-contractual liability of the Community, and provided the standard of State liability.[303] In light of this second and essential requirement, it stated that the critical criterion for establishing a sufficiently serious breach, which was derived from part of the *Schöppenstedt* formula, was "whether the Member State or the Community institution concerned manifestly and gravely disregarded the limits on its discretion"[304].[305] Consequently, the Court referred to the following aspects as being relevant in deciding whether a violation of Community law might be considered sufficiently serious:[306]

> [T]he clarity and precision of the rule breached, the measure of discretion left by that rule to the national or Community authorities, whether the infringement and the damage caused was intentional or involuntary, whether any error of law was excusable or inexcusable, the fact that the position taken by a Community institution may have contributed towards

300 Cf. Van Gerven, 1996, p. 526.
301 *Brasserie/Factortame III* (fn 11), para 51.
302 Cf. Lane, 1996, p. 100.
303 Cf. Convey, 1996, p. 606.
304 *Brasserie/Factortame III* (fn 11), para 55.
305 Cf. Van Gerven, 1996, p. 526.
306 Cf. Tridimas, 1996, pp. 412-413.

> the omission, and the adoption or retention of national measures or practices contrary to Community law.[307]

As a result, it followed that the limits of discretion conferred upon the State at the moment of the violation were evidently crucial to its exposure to liability.[308] Thus, an absence of discretion inevitably led to strict liability.[309] An example held by the ECJ in *Francovich*, and subsequently affirmed in varying case law,[310] was the omission to transpose a directive into national laws within the prescribed time limit constituting *per se* a sufficiently serious breach.[311] Or, as observed by AG Tesauro in his opinion,[312] liability was established in cases where a precise stipulation affording individuals with Community rights was violated and incurred harm; no other aspects had to be taken into account.[313]

The Court did not make an effort to outline the cases in which there was discretion available, and to what degree.[314] However, it was suggested that the exercise of legislative powers implied a broader discretion than the exercise of executive or administrative authority, as exemplified in the jurisprudence[315] of the ECJ.[316] Notwithstanding, the Court observed that a violation of Community law would be considered sufficiently serious, if it endured in light of its judgment determining the violation.[317]

4.2.3 Determination of Breach

The ECJ held that in the case at issue the legislation of both Germany and United Kingdom implicated a wide limit of discretion. Therefore, a right to resti-

---

307 *Brasserie/Factortame III* (fn 11), para 56.
308 Cf. Convey, 1997, p. 607.
309 Cf. Betlem, 1996, (*A. The Ius Commune Regime* section, para 12).
310 Cf. Case C-319/96 *Brinkmann Tabakfabriken GmbH v. Skatteministeriet (Brinkmann)* [1998] ECR I-5255, para 28; cf. Joined Cases C-178/94, C-179/94, C-188/94, C-189/94 & C-190/94 *Erich Dillenkofer & Others v. Bundesrepublik Deutschland (Dillenkofer)* [1996] ECR I-4845, para 29.
311 Cf. Tridimas, 2001, p. 302; cf. Tridimas, 1996, p. 412.
312 Opinion of AG Tesauro in Joined Cases C-46/93 and C-48/93 *Brasserie du Pêcheur SA v. Germany and The Queen v. Secretary of State for Transport, ex parte Factortame Ltd & Others* [1996] ECR I-1029.
313 Cf. ibid, para 80.
314 Cf. Wooldridge & D'Sa, 1996, p. 163.
315 See, e.g. Case C-5/94 *The Queen v. Ministry of Agriculture, Fisheries and Food, ex parte: Hedley Lomas Ltd. (Hedley Lomas)* [1996] ECR I-2553; Case C-392/93 *The Queen v. H. M. Treasury, ex parte British Telecommunications plc. (British Telecom)* [1996] ECR I-1631.
316 Cf. Convey, 1997, p. 607.
317 Cf. Tridimas, 1996, p. 413.

tution could only be established if all three requirements for incurring liability were met.[318]

The Court scrutinized the three requirements in the present case: Of the three requirements, it held that the first requirement was fulfilled, because both Arts. 30 and 52 EEC had direct effect[319] and thus afforded rights to individuals.[320] Regarding the second requirement, it found that its assessment was that of the national court, which was competent, after having been provided guidelines, to "find the facts in the main proceedings and decide how to characterize the breaches of Community law at issue"[321].[322] Nonetheless, the ECJ found it to be valuable to point out a few factors, which the domestic court might take into consideration.[323] According to Oliver, this resulted in the Court engaging in the unusual practice of scrutinizing which of its earlier judgments had been entirely predictable.[324]

In *Brasserie/Factortame III*, the ECJ differentiated between the ban on the labeling of the marketed product and the prohibition of the additives enacted by the German legislation. It held that the German authorities were not exonerated when enacting the labeling ban considering the obvious early jurisprudence[325] laying down the evident incompatibility of such a ban with Community law. However, when it came to the prohibition of additives, such case law, in the words of the Court, did not come into existence before its ruling in the *Beer Purity* case,[326] and thus had not provided such clear direction to the national legislative authorities.[327]

Moving on to the case of Factortame Ltd, the ECJ observed a difference between two types of limitations in the Merchant Shipping Act 1988: while the requirement of nationality was strictly adverse to Community law, the requirements for owners and operators of shipping boats to be resident or domiciled in the United Kingdom were not so plain. These requirements *prima facie* infringed Art. 52 EEC, however, the United Kingdom put forward that in their view they

318 Cf. Oliver, 1997, p. 644.
319 Cf. Case 74/76 *Iannelli & Volpi v. Meroni (Meroni)* [1977] ECR 557, para 2; cf. Case 2/74 *Reyners v. Belgium (Reyners)* [1974] ECR 631, para 32.
320 Cf. Puder, 2000, p. 319.
321 *Brasserie/Factortame III* (fn 11), para 65.
322 Cf. Lane, 1996, p. 100.
323 Cf. Wooldridge & D'Sa, 1996, p. 164.
324 Cf. Oliver, 1997, p. 645.
325 For cases involving breaches of Art. 28 of the EC Treaty, see Case 120/78 *Rewe-Zentral AG v. Bundesmonopolverwaltung für Branntwein (Cassis de Dijon)* [1979] ECR 649; see also Case 193/80 *Commission v. Italy (Italian Vinegar)* [1981] ECR 3019.
326 Cf. Puder, 2000, p. 323.
327 Cf. Oliver, 1997, p. 645.

were justifiable in light of attaining the purposes of the Common Fisheries Policy. The Court had dismissed that reasoning in its judgment in *Factortame II*, however, that did not inevitably suggest that it was plainly unsubstantiated.[328] However, it put forward that if it was to emerge that the United Kingdom had neglected to promptly follow the order of the Court in *Commission v. United Kingdom*[329] and this conduct pointlessly exacerbated the harm, then this would be regarded as constituting a manifest and sufficiently serious breach.[330]

Finally, the ECJ brought its assessment of the three requirements to an end by making reference to national courts for ascertaining the third requirement, the direct link between the infringement by the Member State and the harm sustained by the wronged party.[331]

4.2.4 National Law and Remedies

Thereafter, the Court found that an action in damages brought against the State was to be instituted pursuant to domestic substantive and procedural laws of the Member State on State liability. Moreover, these national laws had to be in compliance with the three requirements laid down by the ECJ, they must not be less favorable than those laws pertaining to corresponding national claims, and they must not make it virtually or exceedingly difficult to apply for and acquire restitution.[332] On that point, it held that domestic laws on State liability which enacted requirements that were less strict continued to be legitimate and applicable.[333]

Consequently, the Court defined two such situations that made the right to reparation exceedingly difficult to exercise and therefore contrary to the law of the Community.[334] It observed that the conditions brought into effect by German law, which necessitated that the action or failure of the legislature in infringement of higher standing domestic rules was referable to an individual situation (*Drittbezogenheit der Amtspflicht*)[335], did not seem to penalize Member State liability actions compared with corresponding national claims, but would effectively make it virtually or exceedingly difficult to acquire restitution for any harm

---

328 Cf. ibid.

329 Case C-246/89 *Commission v. United Kingdom (Merchant Shipping Rules)* [1991] ECR I-4585.

330 Cf. Wooldridge & D'Sa, 1996, p. 164.

331 Cf. Puder, 2000, p. 323.

332 For the so-called minimum standard for the protection of Community rights, see Case C-208/90 *Emmott v. Minister for Social Welfare and Attorney General (Emmott)* [1991] ECR I-4269, para 16; see also *San Giorgio* (fn 126), para 12; *Francovich* (fn 1), para 43.

333 Cf. Lane, 1996, p. 99.

334 Cf. Tridimas, 1996, p. 413.

335 Cf. Art. 839(1) German Civil Code (Bürgerliches Gesetzbuch/BGB) *icw.* Art. 34 German Constitution (Grundgesetz/GG)

sustained following a violation of Community law.[336] In addition, it ruled that the condition instituted by English law of evidence of misfeasance in public office would also effectively make it not possible to secure restitution.[337] Concluding, the ECJ held that in cases concerning Member State liability resulting from a violation of Community law any such limitations had to be revoked.[338]

4.2.5 Role of Fault

Part of the preliminary reference by the *Bundesgerichtshof* was the uncertainty whether fault was a requirement for Member State liability for infringement of Community law.[339] The Court responded to this inquiry by first and foremost stating that the notion of fault was not identical in the numerous legal systems of the Member States. Consequently, the duty to make good the loss or damage inflicted on individuals could not be conditional on any notion of fault "going beyond (...) a sufficiently serious breach of Community law"[340]. Thus, it held that the application of such a further prerequisite would be equivalent to challenge the right to damages under Community law. Nevertheless, in practice, the ECJ acknowledged that both objective and subjective facts related with the notion of fault under a national legal order may be material to the aim of deciding whether or not a particular violation of the law of the Community was sufficiently serious as to establish liability.[341]

4.2.6 Quantum of Damages

Both the English High Court and the German *Bundesgerichtshof* sought preliminary reference as to the measures for determining the amount of damages.[342] In the words of the Court, restitution for harm inflicted on individuals flowing from violations of Community law must be corresponding to the harm suffered, so that the effective protection of their rights was safeguarded.[343]

Subsequently, the ECJ drew attention to its ruling in *Mulder*[344] where it held, pertaining to the non-contractual liability of the Community, that it was a common principle derived from the legal traditions of the Member States that the

336 Cf. Puder, 2000, p. 324.
337 Cf. Tridimas, 1996, p. 413.
338 Cf. Puder, 2000, p. 324.
339 Cf. Oliver, 1997, p. 646.
340 *Brasserie/Factortame III* (fn 11), para 79.
341 Cf. Wooldridge & D'Sa, 1996, p. 165.
342 Cf. Oliver, 1997, p. 647.
343 Cf. Wooldridge & D'Sa, 1996, p. 166.
344 Cf. Joined Cases C-104/89 and C-37/90 *Mulder & Others v. Council and Commission* [1990] ECR I-3061, para 33; see also Joined Cases C-178/94, C-179/94, C-188/94, C-189/94 & C-190/94 *Erich Dillenkofer & Others v. Bundesrepublik Deutschland* [1996] ECR I-4845, para 72.

party harmed should be reasonably diligent as to reduce the extent of the loss or harm it had sustained.[345]

Moreover, the Court heeded the lack of corresponding Community rules and pointed out that the measures laid down by the Member States in their national legal orders were dependent on the limits, which it had set up for the purposes of bringing Member State liability actions.[346]

Next, the ECJ turned to answer the inquiries of both the referring national courts concerning the head of damages and possible constraints thereof. In responding to one of the inquiries referred to by *Bundesgerichtshof*, it ruled once more[347] that the absolute preclusion of profit loss as a head of damage, for which restitution could be granted in the event of an infringement of Community law, could not be permitted because in light of economic and commercial legal proceedings it would render such legal remedy effectively unobtainable.[348]

In its second inquiry the High Court asked about a number of particular heads of damage, all pertaining to losses connected with operating fishing boats. In response, the Court merely established that these were issues determined by domestic law, to be in accordance only with the principles of effectiveness and equivalence. Last, the High Court in addition inquired about exemplary damages, which, under English law, may be granted in the event where public officials conducted themselves in an oppressive, arbitrary or unconstitutional manner.[349] On this matter, the ECJ found that where rules of the national legal order made available exemplary damages, as in the case of English law, such legal actions must be provided for violations of Community law in the same way as they are afforded in comparable cases under national law.[350]

4.2.7 Temporal Effect

The *Bundesgerichtshof* inquired whether reparation must be afforded for the time period preceding March 1987, when the ECJ found, in infringement proceedings under Art. 169 EEC [*ex Art. 226 TEC; now Art. 258 TFEU*], the German acts to be incompatible with Community law.[351] The Court ruled that the duty of a Member State to provide reparation for loss or harm occasioned to individuals for infringements of Community law by the State could not be con-

345 Cf. *Brasserie/Factortame III* (fn 11), para 85; cf. Oliver, 1997, p. 647.
346 Cf. Puder, 2000, p. 325.
347 Cf. Case C-465/93 *Atlanta Fruchthandelsgesellschaft mbH & Others v. Bundesamt für Ernährung und Forstwirtschaft* (Atlanta) [1995] ECR I-3761, para 41.
348 Cf. Wooldridge & D'Sa, 1996, p. 166.
349 Cf. Oliver, 1997, p. 648.
350 Cf. Lane, 1996, p. 100.
351 Cf. Oliver, 1997, p. 648.

strained to damage suffered after the delivery of the decision of the ECJ establishing the violation under consideration.[352] To substantiate its judgment, the Court referred to its previous ruling in in *Waterkeyn*,[353] where it held that the principle of direct effect, conferring enforceable subjective rights to individuals, could not be made conditional on the pronouncement by the ECJ of any decision establishing a violation.[354]

In its conclusion the Court also referred to a request from the German authorities to restrict the temporal effects of the ruling in question. It dismissed the request on grounds that the substantive and procedural provisions of domestic law, while adhering to the requirements responsible for obtaining State liability claims imposed by the ECJ, were qualified to attend matters pertaining to the principle of legal certainty.[355]

4.3 Concluding Observations

The ruling of the Court in *Brasserie and Factortame III* significantly enhanced the principle of Member State liability in the *post-Francovich* period by laying down the universality of the right to damages, establishing the concept of serious breach as a key prerequisite of liability, and shaping State liability on the liability of the institutions of the Community.[356] Liability was only established if the infringement was sufficiently serious, which successively encompassed an inquiry focusing on discretion, *bona fide*, reasonableness and the conduct of associated parties, that is, the Commission and other Member States.[357] For the convenience of the reader, a brief summary of the judgment is depicted in Figure 3.[358]

This landmark ruling, which demonstrated that "the King can do wrong"[359] utilized common principles for defining effective remedies, while permitting the essential definitions of Member State liability to flow from the type of the breach at issue. In principle, the subsequent imposing of liability to such an extent may

---

352 Cf. Wooldridge & D'Sa, 1996, p. 166.
353 Joined Cases 314/81, 315/81, 316/81 and 83/82 *Procureur de la République and Comité national de défense contre l'alcoolisme v. Alex Waterkeyn & Others (Waterkeyn)* [1982] ECR 4337.
354 Cf. ibid, para 16.
355 Cf. Puder, 2000, p. 326.
356 Cf. Tridimas, 2001, p. 302.
357 Cf. ibid.
358 See Figure 3: The Brasserie/Factortame III Judgment at a Glance, p. 55.
359 Granger, 2007, p. 163.

have seemed revolutionary, particularly in those Member States that did not even acknowledge strict liability for acts or omissions of the legislature.[360]

Notwithstanding, acts of the Member States emanated from within the substantive and procedural norms of their national legal orders. Because only matters regarding the legality of Community law were brought up to the ECJ by means of preliminary reference, the national judiciaries determining the facts of each case kept significant privileges, even against the background of the guide of the Court and the principles of effectiveness and equivalence under Community law.[361]

The joined cases of *Brasserie and Factortame III* were the most important, but certainly not the only preliminary reference decisions by the ECJ of the post-*Francovich* period.[362] While they gave a clarification of the requirements for a right to damages, in particular revolving around the sufficiently serious breach test, that was the extent of their powers. To answer the questions that subsequently occupied the *Francovich* case law a look had to be taken elsewhere.[363] And, indeed, all these questions needed to be given form and matter in the forthcoming months and years. The significance and practice of the new tests would have still to be settled in.[364]

---

360 Cf. Puder, 2000, p. 369.
361 Cf. ibid, pp. 369-370.
362 Cf. Caranta, 1995, p. 720.
363 Cf. Dougan, 2011, p. 429.
364 Cf. Lane, 1996, pp. 104-105.

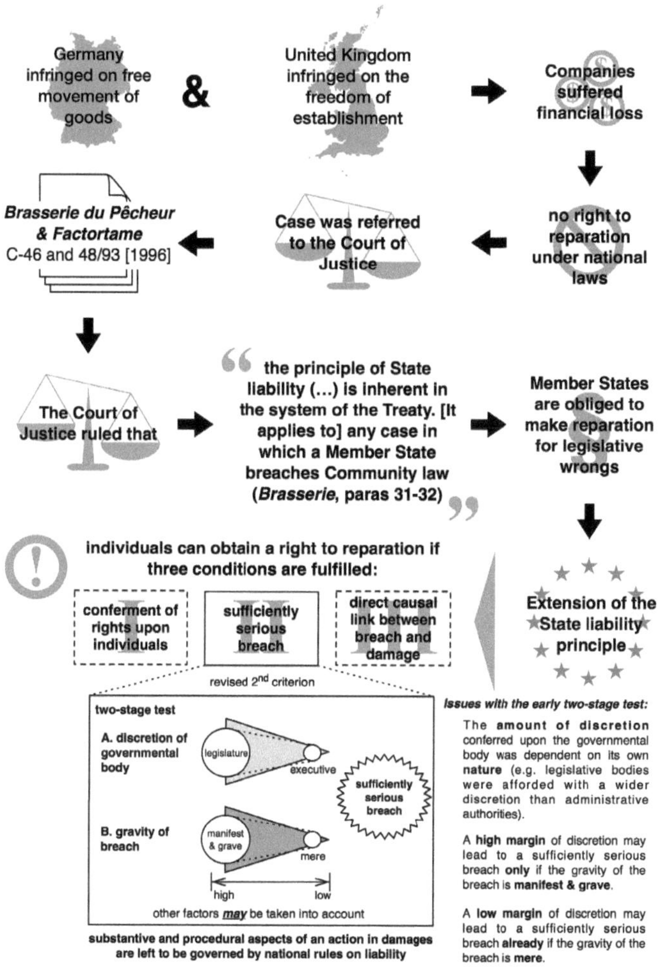

Figure 3: The Brasserie/Factortame III Judgment at a Glance

Figure 3. The main aspects of the judgment in *Brasserie/Factortame III* which expanded the principle of Member State Liability in damages by holding it applicable to any breaches of Community law flowing from Member States or its organs. In *Brasserie/Factortame III* the point of departure was the infringement of the fundamental freedoms by the legislative authorities of Germany and the United Kingdom which as a consequence caused financial loss to the claimants (companies that were denied operating in the respective Member State). As national regimes of non-contractual liability did not afford a right to reparation in such cases, the joined cases were brought before the Court of Justice. The ECJ held that the principle of State liability established in *Francovich* was a universal principle, applying in all cases where a Member State was in breach of Community law. In addition, the European Court revised the conditions for State liability by introducing the requirement of a sufficiently serious breach. This would be assessed by the national courts in a two-stage test based on the discretion of a governmental body and the gravity of the breach.

Source: Own compilation.

5 Development of Case Law After the Brasserie Judgment

5.1 Clarification of the Brasserie Conditions of State Liability

The sections that follow do not address the three requirements of State liability under *Brasserie/Factortame III*[365] and analyze the relevant case law in relation to them in a sequential manner. The reason for this is that case law[366] has shown that the first and third conditions could be, and were, utilized by the European Court as potential instruments in limiting State liability in cases when the second condition was deemed fulfilled. That is why the establishment of a sufficiently serious breach marks the beginning of the following examination into the matter.

5.1.1 Second Condition: Sufficiently Serious Breach

The establishment of the condition of a sufficiently serious breach in *Brasserie/Factortame III* gave an answer to the ongoing question as to whether a standard of strict liability was applicable with regards to the principle of State liability under *Francovich*,[367] or whether, pursuant to the system of non-contractual liability of the Community and other particular non-contractual liability systems of the Member States, there had to be an additional element other than just the infringement of a rule of Community law. The new, more sophisticated assessment would seem to be adequate for complicated fields of policy and law in which State authorities take action, and specifically where they are endowed with a margin of discretion in the exercise of their functions. However, the endeavor of the Court in coming up with such a sophisticated method in *Brasserie/Factortame III* ended up being serpentine. According to Biondi & Farley, the jurisprudence following the judgment had a long way to go in elucidating many of the questions arising from the reasoning of the ECJ in these matters.[368]

5.1.1.1 The Initial Difficulty of Establishing Culpability

Initially, one of the unresolved problems that remained *post-Francovich* was the issue of how to establish culpability of the State in order to establish a serious breach of Community law, which consequently caused significant difficulties in practice.[369] For instance, in *Wagner Miret*,[370] which akin to *Francovich* revolved

---

365 *Brasserie/Factortame III* (fn 11).
366 Cf. Tridimas, 2001, pp. 306 et seqq.
367 *Francovich* (fn 1).
368 Cf. Biondi & Farley, 2009, p. 41.
369 Cf. Uecker, 1994, p. 289.

around the transposition of Directive 80/987,[371] the issue was whether higher management staff also enjoyed protection in the event of insolvency of the employer. The Spanish government took for granted that its national laws were in accordance with the directive when Spain acceded to the Community.[372] In the case, the Court avoided going into detail whether the directive had been implemented correctly and to which governmental authority the breach was attributable to, and instead prompted the Spanish court to interpret national laws in conformance with the directive. Subsequently, it held, *obiter dictum*, that if this was not possible then the plaintiff had to be granted a right to reparation as "an individual's last resort"[373].[374]

Thereby, the ECJ interwove its case law in *Marleasing*[375] and *Francovich*, so that the default of consistent interpretation by national courts would not bring an end to the legal proceedings.[376] Incidentally, before its ruling in *Brasserie/Factortame III*, it would continue to apply the same approach in the cases of *Faccini Dori,*[377] and *El Corte Inglés SA v. Rivero*[378].[379] However, in *Wagner Miret*, as Uecker pointed out, with regard to culpability, the question on behalf of the Spanish government was left unresolved, despite the fact that the Spanish national courts themselves were at odds with whether or not the directive had been implemented properly.[380]

5.1.1.2 The Early Two-Part Approach

Since the judgment of the Court in *Brasserie/Factortame III,* it was laid down that, according to the second *Brasserie* condition, a claim in State liability for the infringement of Community law could not be made unless a sufficiently serious breach was established.[381] Thus, a standard of culpability of the Member State had to be applied, which enforced the duty to prove the existence of a sufficiently serious breach, namely a manifest and grave breach by the omitting governmental body of the extent of its discretion.[382] In the present judgment, the

---

370 *Wagner Miret* (fn 223).
371 Council Directive 80/987/EEC (fn 147).
372 Cf. Uecker, 1994, p. 290.
373 *Wagner Miret* (fn 223), para 23.
374 Cf. ibid, paras 20-22.
375 Case C-106/89 *Marleasing SA v. La Comercial Internacional de Alimentacion SA (Marleasing)* [1990] ECR I-4135.
376 Cf. Foster, 2013, p. 51.
377 *Faccini Dori* (fn 222).
378 *El Corte Inglés* (fn 224).
379 Cf. Kondas, 2008, np; cf. Wolf, 1999, pp. 44-45.
380 Cf. Uecker, 1994, p. 290.
381 Cf. Tridimas, 2001, p. 310.
382 Cf. *Brasserie/Factortame III* (fn 11), paras 55; cf. Anagnostaras, 2007, p. 737.

ECJ gave guidance on a number of factors,[383] which may be taken into consideration with regard to establishing whether the minimum level of seriousness had been met. On that point, and without considering other factors, the issue of discretion afforded to the Member State was in an opposite relationship with the probability of constituting a serious breach. The less discretion was afforded to the authorities of the Member State by the legal order of the Community, the easier it would be to determine that an infringement of Community law was serious.[384]

In 1996, following the seminal decision in *Brasserie/Factortame III*, the Court had opportunity to shed some light on the central unresolved issue of what constituted a sufficiently serious breach of Community law:[385] The case of *British Telecom*[386] dealt with an erroneous transposition of Directive 90/351[387] arising from an incorrect understanding as to the meaning of a provision therein. The ECJ held that the United Kingdom had in fact misread an article, but refused to establish a right in damages, because the Member State was afforded with a wide discretion in the exercise of its legislative functions.[388] It observed that the violation of Community law was not sufficiently serious, as the wording of the article of the directive under consideration was inexact and arguable. Therefore the interpretation derived from it by the United Kingdom and other Member States had not been plainly wrong, because it had been given "in good faith and on the basis of arguments which are not entirely devoid of substance",[389] and in addition there were no clear guidelines from its past jurisprudence.[390]

In a similar fashion, in *Denkavit*,[391] the Court found that an erroneous transposition of Directive 90/435[392] by the legislature of Germany did not give rise to a

---

383 Cf. *Brasserie/Factortame III* (fn 11), paras 56-57; see also chapter 4.2.2 Conditions for Incurring Liability, p. 43.

384 Cf. Tridimas, 2001, pp. 310-311.

385 Cf. Tallberg, 2000, p. 110.

386 Case C-392/93 *The Queen v. H. M. Treasury, ex parte British Telecommunications plc. (British Telecom)* [1996] ECR I-1631.

387 Council Directive 90/531/EEC of 17 September 1990 on the procurement procedures of entities operating in the water, energy, transport and telecommunications sectors (OJ 1990 L 297, pp. 1-48), as repealed by Council Directive 93/38/EEC of 14 June 1993 coordinating the procurement procedures of entities operating in the water, energy, transport and telecommunications sectors (OJ 1993 L 199, pp. 84-138).

388 Cf. *British Telecom* (fn 386), paras 32, 39-40; cf. Craig, 2012, p. 733.

389 *British Telecom* (fn 386), para 43.

390 Cf. *British Telecom* (fn 386), paras 43-45; cf. Oliver, 1997b, p. 664.

391 Joined Cases C-283/94, C-291/94 and C-292/94 *Denkavit International BV & Others v. Bundesamt für Finanzen (Denkavit)* [1996] ECR I-5063.

392 Council Directive 90/435/EEC of 23 July 1990 on the common system of taxation applicable in the case of parent companies and subsidiaries of different Member States (OJ 1990 L 225, pp. 6-10), as repealed by Council Directive 2011/96/EU of 30 November 2011 on the common system of taxation applicable in the case of parent companies and subsidiaries of different Member State (OJ 2011 L 345, pp. 8-16).

sufficiently serious breach, because nearly all other Member States had come to an identical explanation and there was no jurisprudence on the provision in question available.[393]

In *Hedley Lomas*,[394] the administrative authorities of the United Kingdom refused to provide Spain with licenses for exporting live sheep, because Spanish slaughterhouses, in the view of the United Kingdom, were not abiding with the provisions of Directive 74/577[395]. The ECJ held that this mere infringement of Community law was to be considered a sufficiently serious breach, because of the absence of discretion conferred upon Member States under the directive, the clarity of the rules of Community law infringed, and the lack of objectively established grounds for the conduct of the United Kingdom.[396]

Finally, in *Dillenkofer*,[397] a group of holidaymakers made claims in reparation against the German authorities for being in default of its obligation to transpose the Package Travel Directive[398].[399] The ruling of the Court in *Dillenkofer* unified the two groups of substantive conditions for liability advanced in *Francovich* and *Brasserie/Factortame III*.[400] It, referring to *Francovich*, held that where a Member State omitted to take any actions required to attain the aim stipulated by a directive with the prescribed time limit, such conduct was tantamount to a *per se* sufficiently serious breach.[401]

Concluding, from all these cases it could be deduced that discretion was the decisive element that governed the establishment of *Francovich* liability.[402] Where the Member State had no significant discretion in fulfilling its duties emanating from the Treaties, the mere infringement of the law of the Community would be held sufficiently serious to impose liability of the State in damages without having to consider any other elements. In any event, a sufficiently serious infringement of Community law could be established in situations where it

393 Cf. *Denkavit* (fn 391), paras 51-52; cf. Craig, 2012, p. 733.

394 Case C-5/94 *The Queen v. Ministry of Agriculture, Fisheries and Food, ex parte: Hedley Lomas Ltd. (Hedley Lomas)* [1996] ECR I-2553.

395 Council Directive 74/577/EEC of 18 November 1974 on stunning of animals before slaughter (OJ 1974 L 316, pp. 10-11), as repealed by Council Regulation (EC) No 1099/2009 of 24 September 2009 on the protection of animals at the time of killing (OJ 2009 L 303, pp. 1-30).

396 Cf. *Hedley Lomas* (fn 394), paras 28-29; cf. Craig & de Búrca, 2011, p. 250.

397 Joined Cases C-178/94, C-179/94, C-188/94, C-189/94 & C-190/94 *Erich Dillenkofer & Others v. Bundesrepublik Deutschland (Dillenkofer)* [1996] ECR I-4845.

398 Council Directive 90/314/EEC of 13 June 1990 on package travel, package holidays and package tours (OJ 1990 L 158, pp. 59-64), ('Package Travel Directive').

399 Cf. Krümmel, 2009, p. 277.

400 Cf. Dougan, 2004, p. 238.

401 Cf. *Dillenkofer* (fn 397), para 26; see also Case C-319/96 *Brinkmann Tabakfabriken v. Skatteministeriet (Brinkmann)* [1998] ECR I-5255, para 28.

402 Cf. Dougan, 2004, p. 244.

endured in light of a previous judgment by the ECJ declaring an infringement,[403] or established case law existed from which it came apparent that the activities of the Member State amounted to a breach.[404] The Court affirmed the latter in several following cases,[405] which dealt with factual and legal circumstances that had been previously adjudged by the ECJ.[406] Regarding the former, the Court made clear that the existence of such a prior judgment would not be a requirement necessary to constitute a sufficient serious infringement.[407]

5.1.1.3 The Later Objective Criteria Approach

In the aforementioned course of jurisprudence of the ECJ, the element of discretion was the decisive component whether or not State liability could be established.[408] However, as pointed out by Craig, the problem with that approach was that the test was ambiguous because discretion inherently changed depending on the respective nature of State action.[409] As a result, an action by the administration or executive would be tested differently to an action by the legislature.[410] Thus, the ongoing development of the case law indicated that the Court was inclined to withdraw from its early two-part method in establishing a sufficient serious breach on the grounds of availability or lack of a significant level of Member State discretion.[411]

Indeed, in the following judgments of *Haim II*[412] and *Gervais Larsy*,[413] it acknowledged that discretion was not the sole element used in constraining the liability of the State exercising its powers in the interest of the public.[414] In that context, the case of *Haim II* warrants further analysis. It revolved around a den-

403 See generally *Dillenkofer* (fn 397); *Francovich* (fn 1).

404 Cf. *Brasserie/Factortame III* (fn 11), para 57; cf. Dougan, 2004, p. 244.

405 Cf. Case C-429/09 *Günter Fuß v. Stadt Halle (Fuß II)* [2010] ECR I-12167, para 57; see, to that effect, Case C-243/09 *Günter Fuß v. Stadt Halle (Fuß I)* [2010] ECR I-9849; cf. Case C-446/04 *Test Claimants in the FII Group Litigation v. Commissioners of Inland Revenue (FII Group)* [2006] ECR I-11753, paras 214-215; see, to that effect, Case C-35/98 *Verkooijen* [2000] ECR I-4071; Case C-315/02 *Lenz* [2004] ECR I-7063; Case C-319/02 *Manninen* [2004] ECR I-7477; cf. Case C-118/00 *Gervais Larsy v. Institut National d'Assurances Sociales pour Travailleurs Indépendants (Gervais Larsy)* [2001] ECR I-5063, paras 43-44; see, to that effect, Case C-31/92 *Marius Larsy v. Institut National d'Assurances Sociales pour Travailleurs Indépendants (Marius Larsy)* [1993] ECR I-4543.

406 Cf. Craig, 2012, p. 734.

407 Cf. Case C-445/06 *Danske Slagterier v. Germany (Danske Slagerier)* [2009] ECR I-2119, para 114; cf. *Brasserie/Factortame III* (fn 11), para 95; cf. Craig & de Búrca, 2011, p. 248.

408 Cf. Dougan, 2004, pp. 244-245.

409 Cf. Craig, 1998, p. 77.

410 Cf. Lane, 1996, pp. 103-104.

411 Cf. Dougan, 2004, pp. 244-245.

412 Case C-424/97 *Salomone Haim v. Kassenzahnärztliche Vereinigung Nordrhein (Haim II)* [2000] ECR I-5123.

413 Case C-118/00 *Gervais Larsy v. Institut National d'Assurances Sociales pour Travailleurs Indépendants (Gervais Larsy)* [2001] ECR I-5063.

414 Cf. ibid, para 39; cf. *Haim II* (fn 412), paras 41-43; cf. Dougan, 2004, p. 245.

tist with the name of Salomone Haim, who made a claim in damages for the loss of profit that he contended to have sustained following his registration[415] being denied by the association of dental practitioners in violation of Community law. In the course of the proceedings the *Landgericht Düsseldorf* (District Court Düsseldorf) made a preliminary reference to the ECJ inquiring whether, in situations where national administration had no margin of discretion in exercising domestic law contrary to Community law, the sole aspect of not having any discretion in making a decision amounted to a serious breach of Community law.[416]

The Court was quick to point out that in terms of determining the condition of a sufficiently serious breach of Community law, reference must always be made to Community law and not to the national legal order.[417] The margin of discretion, which may have been granted by domestic law upon the national authority occasioning the violation of Community law, in this regard, was irrelevant.[418] Secondly, on the point of discretion, it held that the condition for the assessment of the seriousness of the infringement incurring damage to the claimant was not solely the discretion conferred upon the wrongdoing governmental body, but also the clarity and precision of the rules under scrutiny.[419]

As a consequence, the element of a sufficiently serious breach was isolated from the element of discretion, which invariably differed in extent by virtue of the kind of national body exhibiting it. Thus, it was no longer crucial for the establishment of a right in damages whether the claim was brought against the legislative, the administrative or the judicial bodies of the State, because subsequent to *Haim II* any assessment of the seriousness of infringement would be derived by taking objective standards into account and not merely on the varying extent of discretion that different State bodies might enjoy in a particular legal field.[420]

In that context, judgments on the issue of missing or considerably reduced discretion of a Member State, assessed under objective criteria, in the field of implementing Community laws into the national legal order were, for example, handed down by the ECJ in the following cases:[421]

---

415 See, to that effect, Case C-319/92 *Salomone Haim v. Kassenzahnärztliche Vereinigung Nordrhein (Haim I)* [1994] ECR I-425.
416 Cf. Horspool & Humphreys, 2006, p. 212.
417 Cf. *Haim II* (fn 412), para 40; cf. Horspool & Humphreys, 2006, p. 212.
418 Cf. *Haim II* (fn 412), para 40; cf. Tridimas, 2001, p. 315.
419 Cf. *Haim II* (fn 412), paras 41-43; cf. Anagnostaras, 2001, p. 147.
420 Cf. *Gervais Larsy* (fn 413), para 39; cf. Anagnostaras, 2001, p. 147.
421 Cf. Craig & de Búrca, 2011, p. 250.

In *Stockholm Lindöpark*,[422] a Swedish company running a golf course sought to obtain damages from the Swedish State for alleged losses arising from the Swedish Value Added Tax law, which did not allow for the deduction of input VAT for sport facilities, arguing it to be in violation of the Sixth VAT Directive[423]. The Court ruled that it was obvious that the general exemption imposed by the Swedish legislative authorities could not be based on the Sixth VAT Directive, and the clear language of the directive did not afford the Member with any discretion to make choices in its law making. In such cases, the mere infringement of Community law was enough to amount to a sufficiently serious breach.[424]

In *Schmidberger*,[425] the question first emerged whether human rights would justify what ordinarily would be considered a breach of Community law. In the case at issue, Austrian authorities, considering that it fell in the purview of the fundamental rights of free expression and free assembly, granted environmental campaigners the permission to hold a demonstration on the Brenner motorway, consequently blocking it for nearly 30 hours. Schmidberger, a company dealing with transportation of goods between Germany and Italy, contended that its rights conferred under Community law, in particular the right of free movement of goods, had been infringed. Thus, the company brought action in damages against the Austrian State putting forward that the Austrian authorities were liable in default of omission to prohibit the demonstration.[426]

The ECJ, on a preliminary reference by the *Oberlandesgericht Innsbruck* (Higher District Court of Innsbruck), ruled that the Member States had to safeguard the right to free movement of goods under Community law. Therefore the Austrian authorities would be held liable for their omission to allow access to the motorway, unless they could prove that such conduct was justified.[427] It observed that the right of free movement of goods was not unconditional, and had to be weighed up against other concerns. The same held to be true for the right of free expression.[428] The Court declared that national authorities were afforded with a broad measure of discretion in appraising these two rights. Because the

---

422 Case C-150/99 *Stockholm Lindöpark Aktiebolag v. Sweden (Stockholm Lindöpark)* [2001] ECR I-493.

423 Council Directive 77/388/EEC of 17 May 1977 on the harmonisation of the laws of the Member States relating to turnover taxes - Common system of value-added tax: uniform basis of assessment (OJ 1977 L 145, pp. 1-40), as repealed by Council Directive 2006/112/EC of 28 November 2006 on the common system of value added tax (OJ 2006 L 347, pp. 1-81), ('Sixth VAT Directive').

424 Cf. *Stockholm Lindöpark* (fn 422), para 40; cf. Biondi & Farley, 2009, p. 45.

425 Case C-112/00 *Eugen Schmidberger, Internationale Transporte und Planzüge v. Republik Österreich (Schmidberger)* [2003] ECR I-5659.

426 Cf. *Schmidberger* (fn 425), paras 2, 16-17; cf. Hartley, 2007, p. 145.

427 Cf. *Schmidberger* (fn 425), paras 51 et seqq; cf. Hartley, 2007, p. 145.

428 Cf. *Schmidberger* (fn 425), paras 74, 77-81; cf. Hartley, 2007, p.145.

Austrian authorities followed all appropriate measures to mitigate interference, it concluded that no violation of Community law could be established.[429]

In *AGM-COS.MET*,[430] a public official of the Finnish Ministry of Health denounced the safety of the elevators of the plaintiff, although they conformed to Directive 98/37[431] on work safety. The directive obliged Member States not to prevent, limit, or hinder the putting on the market or into service of such machinery. The ECJ observed that the stipulations of the directive did not afford the Member State with any discretion and the expressions of the Finnish official constituted a sufficiently serious breach.[432]

In *Robins*,[433] the Court ruled that Directive 80/987[434] afforded Member States with a considerable margin of discretion[435] when it came to establishing the degree of protection of entitlement to pension benefits, and it was deemed to not be clear and precise,[436] thus a sufficiently serious breach was unlikely to be established by national courts.[437]

As a final example, in *Synthon*,[438] the ECJ was requested to determine the extent of the discretion afforded to a Member State in regards to an application for mutual recognition of a marketing authorization for a medical product granted by another Member State under Directive 2001/83[439].[440] It observed that the rules in question were clear and precise in nature and only provided a very limited margin of discretion with regards to grounds on which a Member State was authorized to reject a marketing authorization. In the present case, a violation of

---

429 Cf. *Schmidberger* (fn 425); paras 87, 93-94; cf. Hartley, 2007, p.145.

430 Case C-470/03 *AGM-COS.MET Srl v. Suomen valtio and Tarmo Lehtinen (AGM-COS.MET)* [2007] ECR I-2749.

431 Directive 98/37/EC of the European Parliament and of the Council of 22 June 1998 on the approximation of the laws of the Member States relating to machinery (OJ 1998 L 207, pp. 1-46), as repealed by Directive 2006/42/EC of the European Parliament and of the Council of 17 May 2006 on machinery, and amending Directive 95/16/EC (OJ 2006 L 157, pp. 24-86).

432 Cf. *AGM-COS.MET* (fn 430), para 86; cf. Van Dam, 2013, p. 561.

433 Case C-278/05 *Carol Marilyn Robins & Others v. Secretary of State for Work and Pensions (Robins)* [2007] ECR I-1053.

434 Council Directive 80/987/EEC (fn 147).

435 Cf. *Robins* (fn 433), para 74.

436 Cf. ibid, paras 78-80.

437 Cf. Kaczorowska, 2013, p. 320.

438 Case C-452/06 *The Queen, ex parte Synthon BV v. Licensing Authority of the Department of Health (Synthon)* [2008] ECR I-7681.

439 Directive 2001/83/EC of the European Parliament and of the Council of 6 November 2001 on the Community code relating to medicinal products for human use (OJ 2001 L 311, pp. 67-128), as amended by Directive 2012/26/EU of the European Parliament and of the Council of 25 October 2012 amending Directive 2001/83/EC as regards pharmacovigilance (OJ 2012 L 299, pp. 1-4).

440 Cf. Baeyens & Goffin, 2009, p. 105.

the directive was therefore capable of constituting a sufficiently serious breach of Community law.[441]

5.1.2 Third Condition: Direct Causal Link

The third *Brasserie* condition, which had to be attained before a claim in damages could be established under the *Francovich* principle, was the presence of a direct causal link between the infringement of the Member State and the damage sustained by the claimant. The presence of such link was in principle to be established by national courts on the basis of the facts present in the case.[442]

Establishing such a link might, from time to time, turn out to be a truly taxing duty and result in varying difficulties of quantification, especially in cases where there were a number of plausible elements, which as a whole might have been instrumental in causing the damage.[443] However, due to growing concerns that the Member States would be inclined to exploit such an approach in their favor and thus avoid liability, the Court took a more aggressive stance in constricting the requirement by sometimes determining that it itself had enough facts at its disposal to decide whether or not a causal link could be established in a given case.[444]

It was the case of *Brinkmann*,[445] in which the ECJ made use of this privilege for the very first time, consequently constraining the principle of State liability without mitigating its strict policy that non-implementation of a directive is *per se* a sufficiently serious breach.[446] In the case in point, it ruled that although Denmark failed to transpose Directive 79/32[447] within the required time limit, in particular provisions involving the definitions of cigarettes and smoking tobacco, and consequently resulted in an incorrect categorization of the patented tobacco product by the claimant Brinkmann Tabakfabriken as a cigarette for tax reasons, it, nonetheless, did not establish a sufficiently serious breach. The Court held that no direct causal connection between the infringement of Community law and the loss sustained by the claimant could be established. It reasoned

441 Cf. *Synthon* (fn 438), paras 41-46; cf. Baeyens & Goffin, 2009, p. 109.
442 Cf. Tridimas, 2001, p. 310.
443 Cf. Anagnostaras, 2007, p. 737.
444 Cf. Dougan, 2004, pp. 246-247.
445 Case C-319/96 *Brinkmann Tabakfabriken GmbH v. Skatteministeriet (Brinkmann)* [1998] ECR I-5255.
446 Cf. ibid, para 26; cf. Tridimas, 2001, p. 306.
447 Council Directive 79/32/EEC of 18 December 1978 on taxes other than turnover taxes which affect the consumption of manufactured tobacco (OJ 1979 L 10, p. 8), as repealed by Council Directive 95/59/EC of 27 November 1995 on taxes other than turnover taxes which affect the consumption of manufactured tobacco (OJ 1995 L 291, p. 40).

that in spite of the omission to transpose the directive by ministerial dictum, the Danish government conveyed immediate effect to the pertinent rules of the directive. Furthermore, the ECJ concluded that because the product, which was novel and had not existed at the time of implementation of the directive, did not correlate precisely with either definitions of the directive, the categorization made by the Danish government was not significantly irreconcilable with the language or the intent of the directive.[448]

The judgment of the Court in *Brinkmann* demonstrated that where a Member State failed to implement a directive into the national legal order, the national administration may submit as a legitimate justification that, in spite of the omission of transposing activities, they themselves set out to conform with the stipulations of the directive. However, it is put forward that in some circumstances, the stipulations of a directive may not be of such nature that the national administrative bodies are capable of setting right the absence of implementing legislation, in which the State would be held liable by default.[449]

The deliberately liberal stance demonstrated by the ECJ in *Brinkmann* when it came to scrutinizing the conditions for State liability was not present in *Rechberger.*[450] The case of *Rechberger,*[451] akin to *Dillenkofer,* centered on Directive 90/314 on package holidays.[452] The aim of the directive was to keep buyers of package travel away from harm. In line with this, the directive obliged the travel company providing the package holiday to afford adequate security for reimbursement of the amount paid and for sending the traveler to his home country in the case that the company faced bankruptcy.[453] The first issue was the temporal restriction of protection established by the Austrian authorities. The Austrian national laws aimed at putting the directive into effect were relevant for packaged travel arranged after 1 January 1995, the accession date of Austria to the EU,[454] but restricted protection to that with a departure date of 1 May 1995 or later. The Court ruled that the directive afforded Member States

448 Cf. *Brinkmann* (fn 445), paras 29-32; cf. Tridimas, 2001, pp. 305-306.
449 Cf. Tridimas, 2001, p. 306.
450 Cf. ibid, p. 307.
451 Case C-140/97 *Rechberger and Greindl & Others v. Austria (Rechberger)* [1999] ECR I-3499.
452 Cf. Craig, 2012, p. 733.
453 Cf. Tridimas, 2001, p. 307.
454 See, to that effect, Case C-321/97 *Ulla-Brith Andersson and Susannne Wåkerås-Andersson v. Svenska staten (Andersson)* [1999] ECR I-3551; the ECJ had no jurisdiction to rule on matters arising under the EEA agreement prior to its accession to the European Union.

with no discretion in its implementation and thus the temporal restriction enacted in Austrian legislation constituted a serious breach.[455]

The second issue was whether Austrian legislature properly implemented the protection emanating from provisions of the directive and whether a direct causal link between the incorrect implementation of the directive and the sustained damage by the claimants could be established. The ECJ arrived at the conclusion that the directive was not correctly implemented in national law, because it "appears structurally incapable of catering for events in the economic sector in question"[456]. However, since it was not requested to do so, the Court did not rule whether this constituted a serious violation.[457]

Regarding the point of causation, it held that, contrary to the Austrian authorities, the link of causation could not simply be destroyed by the misconduct of the travel agency or by the development of unusual and unexpected circumstances.[458] Craig pointed out on the ruling in *Rechberger* that, although the case at hand involved an incorrect implementation of the same directive, the ECJ came to the same conclusion as in *Dillenkofer*, where the Package Travel Directive had not been implemented, namely that the Member State had committed a sufficiently serious breach.[459]

In the case of *Danfoss*,[460] the Court also held the view that it was needed to give advice on the interpretation of the direct causal link prerequisite,[461] consequently limiting the right to State liability in a similar manner as in *Brinkmann*. The case concerned taxes on mineral oils that were unlawfully levied by the Danish State in breach of Union law pertaining to Directives 92/81 and 92/108[462]. The companies of Danfoss and Sauer-Danfoss, which bought lubricant oils from various Danish oil firms, thus sought reimbursement of the wrongfully levied tax directly from the Danish tax authorities.[463] On a preliminary reference from the *Vestre Landsret* (Western Regional Court), the ECJ held that a

455 Cf. *Rechberger* (fn 451), para 51; cf. Tridimas, 2001, pp. 307-308.
456 *Rechberger* (fn 451), para 62.
457 Cf. Tridimas, 2001, pp. 308-309.
458 Cf. *Rechberger* (fn 451), paras 75-77; cf. Tridimas, 2001, p. 309.
459 Cf. Craig, 2012, p. 733.
460 Case C-94/10 *Danfoss A/S & Others v. Skatteministeriet (Danfoss)*, judgment of 20 October 2011, nyr, paras 35-36.
461 Cf. ibid, paras 12-18.
462 Council Directive 92/12/EEC of 25 February 1992 on the general arrangements for products subject to excise duty and on the holding, movement and monitoring of such products (OJ 1992 L 76, pp. 1-13), as amended by Council Directive 92/108/EEC of 14 December 1992 amending Directive 92/12/EEC on the general arrangements for products subject to excise duty and on the holding, movement and monitoring of such products (OJ 1992 L 390, pp. 124-126), as further repealed by Council Directive 2008/118/EC of 16 December 2008 concerning the general arrangements for excise duty (OJ 2008 L 9, pp. 12-30).
463 Cf. *Danfoss* (fn 460), paras 12-18.

Member State may deny a damages action by a purchasing party to which the unlawful tax had been passed on by the party subject to tax on the basis that no direct link could be established between the imposing of the tax by the State authority and the harm sustained by the purchasing party. However, this only held true on the condition that the purchasing party was allowed to bring a claim against the party subject to tax under national law and presuming that such claim was made not virtually or exceedingly difficult.[464]

According to Beck, it was unexpected that the Court held, in the absence of State liability, that the recovery of the wrongfully levied tax in principle was an issue of procedural law of the national legal order, pursuant to the general principles of effectiveness and equivalence.[465] And indeed, in its decision, the ECJ did not heed the advice of AG Kokott in her opinion in the case that with regard to State liability "any individual can claim compensation for the harm suffered where there is a causal relationship between that harm and a prohibited agreement or practice".[466]

The Court also resorted to limit State liability action by virtue of causality in the more recent case of *Leth*,[467] which centered on the question whether the Environmental Impact Assessment Directive[468] safeguarded individuals against pecuniary loss flowing from reduction of value in property.[469] Notably, it was in previous case law of the ECJ, in *Delena Wells*,[470] where it had already acknowledged liability of the Member State for the omission of conducting an environmental impact assessment by its national authorities.[471] This likelihood of *Francovich*-liability for violations of the directive was in all probability what encouraged the claimant to bring an action in damages before national courts so as to gain reparation for the loss sustained.[472]

In the case, the claimant by the name of Jutta Leth had bought a house in the vicinity of the Vienna International Airport. The airport was subsequently en-

---

464 Cf. ibid, para 39.
465 Cf. Beck, 2012, p. 372.
466 Opinion of AG Kokott in Case C-94/10 *Danfoss A/S & Others v. Skatteministeriet*, judgment of 20 October 2011, nyr, para 82.
467 Case C-420/11 *Jutta Leth v. Republik Österreich and Land Niederösterreich (Leth)*, judgment of 14 March 2013, nyr.
468 Council Directive 85/337/EEC of 27 June 1985 on the assessment of the effects of certain public and private projects on the environment (OJ 1985 L 175, pp. 40-48), as repealed by Directive 2011/92/EU of the European Parliament and of the Council of 13 December 2011 on the assessment of the effects of certain public and private projects on the environment (OJ 2011 L 26, pp. 1-21), ('Environmental Impact Assessment Directive').
469 Cf. Vedder, 2013, np.
470 Case C-201/02 *The Queen, ex parte Delena Wells v. Secretary of State for Transport, Local Government and the Regions (Wells)* [2004] ECR I-723.
471 Cf. ibid, paras 66-69; cf. Prechal, 2008, p. 170.
472 Cf. Vedder, 2013, np.

larged, most likely intensifying the use and the noise it generated. Consequently, the claimant sought damages against the State for property loss, especially arising from aircraft noise. In the proceedings that followed before national courts, it turned out that in regard to the works carried out on the airport, the Austrian authorities had failed to carry out an environmental impact assessment required under the directive.[473]

The Court, in a preliminary ruling referred by the *Oberster Gerichtshof* (Austrian Supreme Court), held that Directive 85/337 conferred the right upon individuals to have the environmental effects of a project assessed, and that pecuniary loss, if it resulted as a direct economic outcome of the effects on the environment of a project carried out by public or private parties, was included by virtue of the protection attained for by the directive.[474]

However, when examining the third *Brasserie* condition, it pointed out that the directive stipulated an environmental impact assessment for particular projects, but, subsequently, did not determine any substantive rules pertaining to environmental affects arising from a project, such as the barring of projects that have adverse effects on the environment. Thus, the ECJ observed that no causal link could be established between the violation of the directive, namely the omission to carry out an economic assessment, and the reduction in the value of the property. The fact that the assessment of environmental impact had not been carried out by national authorities did not, on its own, confer upon individuals the right to damages for solely pecuniary loss arising from devaluation of property.[475]

5.1.3 First Condition: Conferral of Individual Rights

Of the three conditions of State liability, laid down by the Court in *Brasserie/Factortame III*, only the first requirement, that is whether the rule infringed is meant to confer rights to the wronged party, is unequivocally determined by the ECJ. It is that requirement, inherently part of the interpretation of Community law, which is placed entirely under the authority of the Court. The other two conditions may be passed on to the national judiciaries, resting on the facts of the case.[476]

The assessment of whether a provision afforded individuals with rights was a matter of interpretation of Union law. Such an interpretation by the ECJ was

---

473 Cf. ibid.
474 Cf. *Leth* (fn 467), para 44.
475 Cf. ibid, paras 46-48.
476 Cf. Tridimas, 2001, p. 316.

above all carried out with a purpose and in principle with a broader applicability than the principles of national laws such as the German *Schutznorm* doctrine. Still, the Court had not until now established a complete theory of rights in the legal order of the European Community. Consequently, the method of arriving at its conclusions varied to a certain extent from case to case, which the following cases demonstrated:[477]

In *Norbrook Laboratories*,[478] the claimants had requested a marketing authorization for an animal pharmaceutical product with the Ministry of Agriculture, Fisheries and Food.[479] However, the Ministry rejected to issue Norbrook with the requested authorization without first being provided with further details regarding supply, manufacturing and testing of a manufacturing component.[480] Norbrook contested whether the Ministry under Directives 81/851 [481] and 81/852[482] was competent to insist on such information,[483] and consequently claimed that it had sustained damage as a result of the rejected marketing authorization.[484] The ECJ came to the conclusion that these directives did afford applicants with the right to secure a marketing authorization, as the extent of this right was adequately laid down in the directives.[485] However, it was up to the national judiciaries to establish whether the violations at issue had been sufficiently serious to approve liability of the State.[486]

It could be argued that the first condition to fulfill in establishing a State liability claim was not always straightforward to ascertain and it would require a whole range of interpretive techniques in order to come to a conclusion. An express reference to the individual in the language of a rule was not always required, but could suffice.[487] The case of *Peter Paul*[488] served as an example, by indicat-

477 Cf. Lock, 2012, p. 1689.
478 Case C-127/95 *Norbrook Laboratories Ltd v. Ministry of Agriculture, Fisheries and Food (Norbrook Laboratories)* [1998] ECR I-1531.
479 Cf. Douglas-Scott, 2002, p. 328.
480 Cf. Tridimas, 2001, p. 316.
481 Council Directive 81/851/EEC of 28 September 1981 on the approximation of the laws of the Member States relating to veterinary medicinal products (OJ 1981 L 317, pp. 1-15), as repealed by Directive 2001/82/EC of the European Parliament and of the Council of 6 November 2001 on the Community code relating to veterinary medicinal products (OJ 2001 L 311, pp. 1-66).
482 Council Directive 81/852/EEC of 28 September 1981 on the approximation of the laws of the Member States relating to analytical, pharmaco-toxicological and clinical standards and protocols in respect of the testing of veterinary medicinal products (OJ 1981 L 317, pp. 16-18), as repealed by Directive 2001/82/EC of the European Parliament and of the Council of 6 November 2001 on the Community code relating to veterinary medicinal products (OJ 2001 L 311, pp. 1-66).
483 Cf. Tridimas, 2001, p. 316.
484 Cf. Douglas-Scott, 2002, p. 328.
485 Cf. *Norbrook Laboratories* (fn 478), para 108; cf. Tridimas, 2001, p. 316.
486 Cf. *Norbrook Laboratories* (fn 478), para 112; cf. Douglas-Scott, 2002, p. 328.
487 Cf. Lock, 2012, p. 1690.

ing that it was not sufficient, if a directive, pertaining to the scope of protection under it, merely referred to individuals in its preamble, but did not additionally specify them in any particular stipulations.[489]

In the case, the Court held that the Banking Directives[490] did not prevent a Member State from determining that the activities of a national banking supervision authority were to be carried out in the general interest only, barring claims for damages by individuals resulting from inadequate supervision on behalf of the authority.[491] Consequently, the Banking Directives did not provide a conferral of rights on depositors in case their accounts were not available as a consequence of inadequate supervision, which, as a matter of fact, was aimed at protecting the stability of financial markets.[492]

The judgment of the ECJ in *Peter Paul* had been strongly condemned, and according to Biondi & Farley, quite rightfully so. The interpretation of the individual rights prerequisite was doubtless much more limited than in earlier cases. A likely rationale for such a narrow interpretation could be the unwillingness of the Court to make local authorities, in the sensitive field of banking supervision, subject to litigation, resulting in the liability of the State for the failure of the bank.[493]

A similar line of reasoning was put forward by the ECJ in *Ten Kate Holding*,[494] where the plaintiffs contended that they had sustained damages occasioned by the Commission under Decision 94/381[495] for its omission to authorize safety

488 Case C-222/02 *Peter Paul & Others v. Bundesrepublik Deutschland (Peter Paul)* [2004] ECR I-9425.

489 Cf. Prechal, 2008, p. 167.

490 First Council Directive 77/780/EEC of 12 December 1977 on the coordination of the laws, regulations and administrative provisions relating to the taking up and pursuit of the business of credit institutions (OJ 1977 L 322, pp. 30-37); Council Directive 89/299/EEC of 17 April 1989 on the own funds of credit institutions (OJ 1989 L 124, pp. 16-20); and Second Council Directive 89/646/EEC of 15 December 1989 on the coordination of laws, regulations and administrative provisions relating to the taking up and pursuit of the business of credit institutions and amending Directive 77/780/EEC (OJ 1989 L 386, pp. 1-13), as repealed by Directive 2000/12/EC of the European Parliament and of the Council of 20 March 2000 relating to the taking up and pursuit of the business of credit institutions (OJ 2000 L 126, pp. 1-59); Directive 94/19/EC of the European Parliament and of the Council of 30 May 1994 on deposit-guarantee schemes (OJ 1994 L 135, pp. 5-14), as amended by Directive 2009/14/EC of the European Parliament and of the Council of 11 March 2009 amending Directive 94/19/EC on deposit-guarantee schemes as regards the coverage level and the payout delay (OJ 2009 L 68 pp. 3-7), ('Banking Directives').

491 Cf. *Peter Paul* (fn 488), para 47; cf. Reich, 2005, p. 326.

492 Cf. *Peter Paul* (fn 488), para 50; cf. Reich, 2005, p. 326.

493 Cf. Biondi & Farley, 2009, p. 37.

494 Case C-511/03 *Staat der Nederlanden (Ministerie van Landbouw, Natuurbeheer en Visserij) v. Ten Kate Holding Musselkanaal BV & Others (Ten Kate)* [2005] ECR I-8979.

495 Commission Decision 94/381/EC of 27 June 1994 concerning certain protection measures with regard to bovine spongiform encephalopathy and the feeding of mammalian derived protein (OJ 1994 L 172, pp. 23-24), as repealed by Commission Regulation (EC) No

measures pertaining to bovine spongiform encephalopathy (BSE). Thus, they sought reparation from the Netherlands on the basis that the State had been mistaken in not having initiated proceedings against the Commission under Art. 232 TEC [*now Art. 265 TFEU*]. The Court held, on a request for a preliminary ruling by the *Hoge Raad* (Dutch Supreme Administrative Court), that the Community legal order did not oblige a Member State to initiate proceedings against Community institutions, such as for annulment of an act or for failure to act, in the best interest of its citizens, although, it did not, generally, prevent national legislation from establishing such a duty.[496] In its ruling, it even warned the Member States of initiating such proceedings and thus setting off liability claims, because doing so could result in an avalanche of claims, some of which would be plainly unjustified, and therefore compromise the correct operation of the Court of Justice.[497]

Sometimes the line of reasoning of the ECJ was not fully consistent and in part contradictory.[498] In more recent case law, it advanced in the field of public procurement. It was in *Stadt Graz v. Strabag*,[499] when the Court first ruled that the provisions of Directive 89/665[500] prohibited national laws from making reparation of loss or damage conditional upon fault, referring to the principle of effectiveness, and therewith establishing a regime of strict liability.[501] Whereas in *Combinatie Spijker*,[502] it subsequently observed that the same provisions of the directive referred to the principle of State liability, and therefore held that it was enshrined in the directive that Member States must enact rules for the possibility of granting reparation due to violation of Community law on the award of public contracts. However, contrary to the ruling in *Stadt Graz*, the ECJ ruled that the directive in question neither specified the conditions under which an awarding authority could be held liable in the event of a breach of Community

1326/2001 of 29 June 2001 laying down transitional measures to permit the changeover to the Regulation of the European Parliament and of the Council (EC) No 999/2001 laying down rules for the prevention, control and eradication of certain transmissible spongiform encephalopathies (OJ 2001 L 177, pp. 60-67).

496 Cf. *Ten Kate* (fn 494), paras 27-28, 30-32; cf. Horspool & Humphreys, 2006, p. 215.

497 Cf. *Ten Kate* (fn 494), para 31; cf. Biondi & Farley, 2009, pp. 37-38.

498 Cf. Rihs & Steiner, 2013, p. 142.

499 Case C-314/09 *Stadt Graz v. Strabag AG & Others (Stadt Graz)* [2010] ECR I-8769.

500 Council Directive 89/665/EEC of 21 December 1989 on the coordination of the laws, regulations and administrative provisions relating to the application of review procedures to the award of public supply and public works contracts (OJ 1989 L 395, pp. 33-35), as amended by Directive 2007/66/EC of the European Parliament and of the Council of 11 December 2007 amending Council Directives 89/665/EEC and 92/13/EEC with regard to improving the effectiveness of review procedures concerning the award of public contracts (OJ 2007 L 335, pp. 31-46).

501 Cf. *Stadt Graz* (fn 499), para 39; cf. Wurmnest & Heinze, 2011, pp. 64-65.

502 Case C-568/08 *Combinatie Spijker Infrabouw/De Jonge Konstruktie & Others v. Provincie Drenthe (Combinatie Spijker)* [2008] ECR I-12655.

law, nor how to determine the amount of compensation. It continued to observe that the conditions for Member State liability pertaining to an infringement of Community law were laid down in its existing jurisprudence, for example in *Francovich*.[503]

Notably, in the recent case of *Danske Slagterier*,[504] where Germany had disregarded its duty under a number of directives pertaining to the import of pork originating from non-neutered male pigs and thus refused countless shipments of pork from the State of Denmark,[505] the Court put forward a more tolerant approach than it had expressed in *Peter Paul*, by touching upon the point that Directives 64/433[506] and 89/662[507] had to be considered as substantiation of the rights afforded under Art. 23 TEC [*ex Art. 28 TFEU*], concluding that the rules at issue were considered to be conferring rights on individuals.[508]

As a final example, the two cases of *Fuß I*[509] and *Fuß II*,[510] between Günter Fuß, a firefighter, and his employer, the City of Halle, centering on the implementation of Germany of the Directive 2003/88[511] shall be mentioned.[512] In both cases, the ECJ referred to a specific mention of the health and safety of workers in language of the Working Time Directive to adjudicate that the minimum stipulations included therein did provide workers with rights.[513]

5.2 Deference to National Courts

Apart from cases where the Court laid down the seriousness of a breach, there also existed cases in which it passed the determination whether a breach was

503 Cf. ibid, paras 86-87; cf. Rihs & Steiner, 2013, pp. 141-142.
504 Case C-445/06 *Danske Slagterier v. Germany (Danske Slagterier)* [2009] ECR I-2119.
505 Cf. ibid, paras 11 et seqq.
506 Council Directive 64/433/EEC of 26 June 1964 on health problems affecting intra-Community trade in fresh meat (OJ 121, pp. 2012-2032), as repealed by Directive 2004/41/EC of the European Parliament and of the Council of 21 April 2004 repealing certain Directives concerning food hygiene and health conditions for the production and placing on the market of certain products of animal origin intended for human consumption (OJ 2004 L 175, pp. 33-44).
507 Council Directive 89/662/EEC of 11 December 1989 concerning veterinary checks in intra-Community trade with a view to the completion of the internal market (OJ 1989 L 395, pp. 13-22), as amended by Directive 2004/41/EC of the European Parliament and of the Council of 21 April 2004 repealing certain directives concerning food hygiene and health conditions for the production and placing on the market of certain products of animal origin intended for human consumption (OJ 2004 L 157, pp. 33-44).
508 Cf. *Danske Slagterier* (fn 504), paras 22, 24; cf. Lock, 2012, pp. 1690-1691.
509 Case C-243/09 *Günter Fuß v. Stadt Halle (Fuß I)* [2010] ECR I-9849.
510 Case C-429/09 *Günter Fuß v. Stadt Halle (Fuß II)* [2010] ECR I-12167.
511 Directive 2003/88/EC of the European Parliament and of the Council of 4 November 2003 concerning certain aspects of the organisation of working time (OJ 2003, L 299, pp. 9-19), ('Working Time Directive').
512 Cf. Tomkin, 2012, p. 1423.
513 Cf. *Fuß II* (fn 510), para 49; cf. *Fuß I* (fn 509), para 65; cf. Lock, 2012, p. 1689.

sufficiently serious on to national judiciaries. It was inclined to do so where there was no evident solution whether there had been such a violation in regards to the conditions laid down in *Brasserie/Factortame III*.

For instance, in *Evans*,[514] the claimant contended that the United Kingdom had incorrectly transposed Directive 84/5[515] regarding mandatory liability insurance for motor vehicles, in particular the stipulations pertaining to damage occasioned by unidentified vehicles. The ECJ ruled that the national court was entrusted with the task of establishing, in view of the *Brasserie/Factortame III* factors, whether there had been an incorrect transposition and if so, whether the violation arising out of it was sufficiently serious to establish liability of the State.[516]

In the recently decided case of *DEB*,[517] the Court was also facing an imbroglio over the matter whether the restriction of the fundamental right to access to courts constituted a sufficiently serious breach. The claimant, a German limited company dealing with the supply of energy, contended that it had become insolvent due to the omission of Germany to implement Directive 98/30[518] and its successor, Directive 2003/55[519], which were intended to liberalize the market for gas and electricity.[520]

In fact, in *Commission v. Germany*,[521] the ECJ had previously ruled that Germany had defaulted on its obligation to implement these directives within the required timeframe. This postponed transposition of the directives resulted in the insolvency of the company, because it was unable to maintain its commer-

---

514 Case C-63/01 *Samuel Sidney Evans v. Secretary of State for the Environment, Transport and the Regions and Motors Insurers' Bureau (Evans)* [2003] ECR I-14447.

515 Second Council Directive 84/5/EEC of 30 December 1983 on the approximation of the laws of the Member States relating to insurance against civil liability in respect of the use of motor vehicles (OJ 1984 L 8, pp. 17-20), as repealed by Directive 2009/103/EC of the European Parliament and of the Council of 16 September 2009 relating to insurance against civil liability in respect of the use of motor vehicles, and the enforcement of the obligation to insure against such liability (OJ 2009 L 263, pp. 11-31).

516 Cf. *Evans* (fn 514), paras 84-85; cf. Craig, 2012, p. 734.

517 Case C-279/09 *DEB Deutsche Energiehandels- und Beratungsgesellschaft mbH v. Bundesrepublik Deutschland (DEB)* [2010] ECR I-13849.

518 Directive 98/30/EC of the European Parliament and of the Council of 22 June 1998 concerning common rules for the internal market in natural gas (OJ 1998 L 204, p. 1), as repealed by Directive 2003/55/EC of the European Parliament and of the Council of 26 June 2003 concerning common rules for the internal market in natural gas (OJ 2003 L 176, pp. 57–78).

519 Directive 2003/55/EC of the European Parliament and of the Council of 26 June 2003 concerning common rules for the internal market in natural gas and repealing Directive 98/30/EC (OJ 2003 L 176, pp. 57–78), as repealed by Directive 2009/73/EC of the European Parliament and of the Council of 13 July 2009 concerning common rules for the internal market in natural gas (OJ 2009 L 211, pp. 94–136).

520 Cf. Hess, 2012, p. 166.

521 Case C-64/03 *Commission v. Germany* [2004] ECR I-3551.

cial operations due to lack of access to the gas market. Thus, DEB brought an action for damages by relying on the principle of State liability under Community law.[522] However, its application for legal aid was denied, because German law[523] precluded legal persons from receiving such relief, unless there was public interest in such litigation. On appeal, the *Kammergericht* (Higher Regional Court) made a reference for a preliminary ruling to the Court asking whether Community law, and in particular, the principle of effectiveness, precluded German national procedural rules on legal aid preventing a legal person to gain access to a court.[524] However, the decision of the Second Chamber of the Court was rather opaque.[525] While emphasizing the importance of the principle of effectiveness and the constitutional right of access to justice, it, by only giving general guidelines, focused on a case-by-case approach and left the referring court with the responsibility of determining whether the requirements for granting legal aid amounted to a restriction of the fundamental right to access to courts.[526] As a conclusion it can be said that the case served as an example of the difficulties arising in practice from the private enforcement of European rights, which, according to Hess, may call for a novel interpretation of national procedural rules.[527]

5.3 Compatibility of National Rules of Procedure

Although *Brasserie/Factortame III* contributed some direction on the issue of which situations liability of the State could be established, many undecided matters were passed on to be resolved by rules of the national legal systems, in accordance with the general principles of effectiveness and equivalence.[528] For instance, some issues, which were subject to the rules of domestic law were: the domestic court of competent jurisdiction, procedural rules (time limits, rules of evidence) and the demarcation of liability between the central and decentralized bodies, for example as in a federation,[529] but also matters of causation, Member State discretion, as well as assessment and mitigation of damages.[530] This, as a consequence, implied that the Court was requested to adjudge

522 Cf. Kaczorowska, 2013, p. 225.
523 Cf. Art. 116(2) German Civil Procedure Code (Zivilprozessordnung/ZPO).
524 Cf. Hess, 2012, pp. 166-167.
525 Cf. ibid, p. 167.
526 Cf. *DEB* (fn 517), paras 59-60; cf. Kaczorowska, 2013, p. 225; cf. Hess, 2012, p. 167.
527 Cf. Hess, 2012, p. 167.
528 Cf. Craig & de Búrca, 2011, p. 251.
529 Cf. Widdershoven, 2002, p. 300.
530 Cf. Craig, 2012, p. 736.

whether specific national laws limiting the applicability of State liability were in conformity with Community law.[531]

5.3.1 Time Limits and Rules of Evidence

Regarding the issue of time limits imposed by national procedural laws on State liability claims, this could be illustrated by the three cases[532] stemming from the legal dispute in *Francovich*.[533] The case of *Palmisani*[534] provided a good example: Mrs Palmisani was denied reparation under Italian law, because she had not established her damage claim for the omission of the Italian State to transpose Directive 80/987 within the time limit of one-year required by national legislation. The general time frame for domestic cases pertaining to non-contractual liability, however, was five years. First, the ECJ scrutinized if the principle of effectiveness had been encroached. In *Palmisani*, it ruled that the one-year time frame was in conformity with the principle, because it did not make obtaining the restitution exceedingly difficult.[535] Second, turning to the principle of equivalence, the Court set the compensation regime for harm occasioned by late transposition of the Directive side by side with the national regime of non-contractual liability. However, it ultimately became aware that it did not have enough facts to determine whether the two systems were equivalent.[536] In the end, the ECJ entrusted the national court to find out whether the principle of equivalence had been impinged.[537]

Regarding rules of evidence under national law, the Court held in the case of *Dounias*[538] that such rules would not be precluded, if they were in conformity with the principles of effectiveness and equivalence, thus, witness evidence in cases of State liability was permissible only in exceptional cases.[539]

---

531 Cf. ibid.

532 See generally Case C-373/95 *Frederica Maso & Others and Graziano Gazzeta & Others v. Istituto nazionale della previdenza sociale and Repubblica Italiana (Maso)* [1997] ECR I-4051; Case C-261/95 *Rosalba Palmisani v. Istituto nazionale della previdenza sociale (Palmisani)* [1997] I-4025; Joined Cases C-94/95 and C-95/95 *Danila Bonifaci & Others and Wanda Berto & Others v. Istituto nazionale della previdenza sociale (Bonifaci & Berto)* [1997] I-3969.

533 Cf. Craig, 2012, p. 736.

534 Case C-261/95 *Rosalba Palmisani v. Istituto nazionale della previdenza sociale (Palmisani)* [1997] I-4025.

535 Cf. *Palmisani* (fn 534), paras 27-29.

536 Cf. *Palmisani* (fn 534), paras 36-38; cf. Craig, 2012, p. 736.

537 Cf. *Palmisani* (fn 534), paras 33, 40; cf. Craig & de Búrca, 2011, p. 252.

538 Case C-228/98 *Kharalambos Dounias v. Minister for Economic Affairs (Dounias)* [2000] ECR I-577.

539 Cf. ibid, paras 70-71.

5.3.2 Demarcation of Liability Between State Bodies

By now, it was apparent from the jurisprudence of the ECJ that the *Francovich* remedy in damages could be applied relating to infringements of Community law occasioned by the legislative, judicial, and executive branches of government. However, this resulted in the issue that it was not always straightforward to designate in which function the State had occurred a particular infringement.[540] On that point, a more complicated problem could arise when taking into account the decision in *Constanzo*,[541] in which the Court pointed out that all domestic judicial and administrative authorities were under the obligation to comply with directives with direct effect and disapply conflicting domestic laws.[542] Thus, it followed that in light of *Brasserie/Factortame III* it could have also been implied that the breach of Community law stemmed from the failure of the executive to abide by rather than to disapply national laws, as opposed to the legislature. However, if the ECJ had indeed followed such an approach in its judgment, then this ultimately would have led to the problem of infringement of constitutional principles of the Member States, *in casu* the principle of legal certainty in Germany (*Rechtsstaatlichkeitsprinzip)*.[543]

The Court, in trying to remedy the prevalent problem, provided some guidelines in its case law concerning the designation of liability between the legislative and the administrative authorities. In *Brinkmann*, regarding the transposition of directives, it held that that an administrative body could be held liable for its conduct, if the infringement was resulting from the omission to enforce a directly effective provision of Community law, disapplying any national law opposed to it. Therefore, it could be asserted that any harm flowing from the inaction of the national administration to make compatible the wording of inconsistent national laws with the stipulations of Community law should be attributed to the respective administrative body. It followed that the activities of the national legislation could only be held responsible for the loss of the claimant, when the damage flowed directly from an infringement by the legislature without the intervention of an administrative body, and when the breach pertained to stipulations of Community law without direct effect, and there was no means of interpreting the national law in light of Community law.[544]

Still, the pinpointing of the exact authority of the State a particular infringement was attributed to in the first place would only be critical if it had consequences

---

540 Cf. Anagnostaras, 2001, p. 142.
541 Case 103/88 *Fratelli Costanzo SpA v. Comune di Milano (Constanzo)* [1989] ECR 1839.
542 Cf. ibid, paras 31-33.
543 Cf. Uecker, 1994, p. 290.
544 Cf. Anagnostaras, 2001, p. 144.

for assessing the standard of culpability that will be necessary for the compensation of damages to the claimant.[545] Only such circumstances entailed determining the State entity accountable to carry out the compensation. Undeniably the ECJ did not want to incur a lengthy debate as to which part of the State was actually accountable for the violation in such cases. Thus, it simply held that the Member State itself would be responsible, and it would be at the discretion of the Member State to subsequently designate the damage to specific bodies of the State.[546]

In *Konle*,[547] the Court had the chance to pronounce whether the State was in fact required to provide reparation to individuals for illegitimate actions inflicted by specific centralized and decentralized public entities. Considering the designation of liability between the federal State and federated State entities, it laid down that the duty to provide reparation to a party at loss was triggered without the State involved being permitted to "plead the distribution of powers and responsibilities between the bodies that exist in its national legal order to free itself from liability on this basis"[548].[549] Thus, the Member State could not exploit such a system of government to discharge itself from responsibility. Apart from that requirement, Community law did not mandate Member States to amend the allocation of functions between public bodies in their territory, as long as the general principles of Community law were complied with. For instance, a federal Member State was not required to afford restitution specifically through federal authorities.[550]

This train of thought was expanded in *Haim II*.[551] In this case, the ECJ affirmed its judgment in *Konle* and furthermore ruled that the rationale therein could also be employed for Member States without a federal system of government, where particular legislative or administrative activities were delegated to territorial entities with a specific degree of institutional and functional independence, or to any other entity of public law legally separate from the State. Neither did Community law exclude a body of public law besides the State itself from being accountable to provide reparation for damage inflicted by actions taken in violation of Community law.[552]

---

545 Cf. ibid, p. 143.
546 Cf. Craig, 2012, p. 735.
547 Case C-302/97 *Klaus Konle v. Austria (Konle)* [1999] ECR I-3099.
548 Ibid, para 62.
549 Cf. Anagnostaras, 2001, p.141.
550 Cf. Craig, 2012, p. 735.
551 Cf. *Haim II* (fn 412), para 38; cf. Craig, 2012, p. 735.
552 Cf. *Haim II* (fn 412), paras 31-32; cf. Craig, 2012, p. 735.

5.3.3 Additional Requirements for State Liability

When Member States imposed additional requirements for bringing successful claims in damages under State liability, the Court was quick to establish that these limiting requirements were incompatible with Community law, in particular with the principles of effectiveness and equivalence.[553]

For instance, in *AGM-COS.MET*, it observed that a rule of Finnish national law making the right to reparation for any damage other than person or property damage conditional on whether it emanated from a criminal act, from action of a public authority, or when there were especially serious grounds for granting reparation, was incompatible with Community rules.[554]

Moreover, in *Fuß II*, the Court was again requested to determine whether Union law prevented national legislature from establishing additional requirements for damages claims pertaining to infringements of Union law, particularly with regard to proving fault caused by the employer, and the duty to make a prior application to the employer to secure compensation for overtime.[555] In its judgment the ECJ ruled that although Union law did not refuse State liability claims based on conditions that were less constraining than the ones of Union law,[556] it excluded the enforcement of any supplementary requirements under national law.[557]

5.3.4 Choice of Legal Remedies and Conduct of Claimant

The principles of effectiveness and equivalence have also been employed to attain some uniformity in the remedial actions provided by national legislation. As a result of the stipulations of Community law, rules on procedure for securing reparation for damages have, to a large part, been adapted, put aside or annulled to make sure that individuals could obtain pertinent legal relief.[558] However, in principle, the Court also acknowledged that some constraints on obtaining legal relief under national laws were likely to be permissible,[559] in such events, it continued to regard if the State could be held responsible under the *Francovich* principle.[560]

---

553 Cf. Craig & de Búrca, 2011, p. 251.
554 Cf. *AGM-COS.MET* (fn 430), para 91; cf. Craig & de Búrca, 2011, p. 251.
555 Cf. *Fuß II* (fn 510), para 64.
556 Cf. Case C-524/04 *Test Claimants in the Thin Cap Group Litigation v. Commissioners of Inland Revenue (Thin Cap)* [2007] ECR I-2107, para 115; cf. *Brasserie/Factortame III* (fn 11), para 66.
557 Cf. *Fuß II* (fn 510), para 66; cf. Tomkin, 2012, p. 1430.
558 Cf. Kaczorowska, 2013, p. 333.
559 Cf. *Danske Slagterier* (fn 504), paras 63-64.
560 Cf. Craig & de Búrca, 2011, p. 253.

Since, the principle of Member State liability was independent in nature, individuals retained the freedom to resort to other remedial actions, although, generally they could always choose to bring action against the Member State to exercise the ancillary right to reparation rather than enforcing their primary rights.[561] On that point, Prechal opined that a subject might benefit more from the exercise of national rules complying with to Community law, or their direct effect than by compensation of damages flowing from State liability.[562]

Still, in light of the availability of other legal remedies, the question inevitable emerged whether a damages claim based on State liability of the Member State could be denied due to inaction of the claimant in exercising them to avert the incidence of damage. The mitigation principle, established in *Brasserie*,[563] was a powerful influence against granting claims in damages to plaintiffs, which could be averted, if they instead had based their claims on the supremacy of the legal order of the Community, direct effect or the duty of consistent interpretation.[564]

The ECJ had ample opportunity to deal with the matter in question. First, in *Stockholm Lindöpark*, it cast aside the reasoning that a claim in State liability should be excluded, because the claimant could bring action before the national courts on the grounds of a directly effective provision of Community law.[565] Followed by *Metallgesellschaft,*[566] where the Court disregarded the reasoning of the United Kingdom that the claimants should have established their claims on the direct effect of Community law, rather than settling tax charges first and contesting them afterwards.[567] Moreover, in the more recent case of *Transportes Urbanos*,[568] it was confronted with the question as to whether Community law allowed Spanish national law to mandate that all national legal remedies

561 Cf. Leczykiewicz, 2010, p. 263.
562 Cf. Prechal, 2006, p. 301.
563 Cf. *Brasserie/Factortame III* (fn 11), para 85; for further discussion, see Wattel, P. J. (2008). National procedural autonomy and effectiveness of EC law: Challenge the charge, file for restitution, sue for damages? *Legal Issues of Economic Integration, 35*(2), 109–132; and Anagnostaras, G. (2001). State liability and alternative courses of action: How independent can an autonomous remedy be? In P. Eeckhout, & T. Tridimas (Eds.), *Yearbook of European Law 2001* (pp. 355-383). Oxford: Oxford University Press; Oliver, P. (1998) State liability in damages following Factortame III: A remedy seen in context. In J. Beatson, & T. Tridimas (Eds.), *New Directions in European Public Law* (pp. 49-61). Oxford: Hart Publishing.
564 Cf. Leczykiewicz, 2010, p. 263.
565 Cf. *Stockholm Lindöpark* (fn 422), para 35; cf. Craig & de Búrca, 2011, p. 253.
566 Joined Cases C-397/98 and C-410/98 *Metallgesellschaft & Others and Hoechst v. Commissioners of Inland Revenue and H. M. Attorney General (Metallgesellschaft)* [2001] ECR I-1727.
567 Cf. ibid, paras 99-107; cf. Craig & de Búrca, 2011, p. 240.
568 Case C-118/08 *Transportes Urbanos y Servicios Generales SAL v. Administración del Estado (Transportes Urbanos)* [2010] ECR I-635.

must be exhausted before a damages claim for the infringement of Community law could be brought before national courts. The ECJ held on the ground of the circumstances that the Spanish rules of procedure infringed the principle of equivalence, because the exhaustion of remedies did not also apply to national claims in reparation for violation of the Spanish Constitution.[569]

In these and subsequent cases,[570] the Court, despite what could be generally presumed from its ruling in *Brasserie/Factortame III*,[571] took the stance that it would be in conflict with the principle of effectiveness to compel those who have sustained harm to methodically make use of every legal relief obtainable to them, as this would either be an unreasonable demand or involve some form of complications.[572] Thus, it could be established that Community law did not compel individuals to resort to other remedial actions. Although there might be circumstances in which the omission to exercise other legal remedies will result in ramifications for the claim for reparation, even then the principle of State liability persisted to be a general principle because of its residual nature: it caught all occurrences in which the individual was not successful in depending upon other remedial actions or where no such actions were available under national laws.[573]

569 Cf. Kaczorowska, 2013, p. 330.

570 Cf. *Fuß II* (fn 510), para 78; cf. *Danske Slagterier* (fn 504), para 63; cf. Case C-201/05 *Test Claimants in the CFC and Dividend Group Litigation v. Commissioners of Inland Revenue (CFC Dividend)* [2008] I-2875, para 128; cf. Case C-524/04 *Test Claimants in the Thin Cap Group Litigation v. Commissioners of Inland Revenue (Thin Cap)* [2007] ECR I-2107, para 125; cf. *Metallgesellschaft* (fn 566), para 106.

571 Cf. *Brasserie/Factortame III* (fn 11), paras 84-85.

572 Cf. European Commission, 2009, p. 13.

573 Cf. Leczykiewicz, 2010, p. 264.

6 Liability for Judicial Breaches of European Law

6.1 Extension of the Francovich Principle in Köbler v. Austria

6.1.1 Factual and Procedural Background

Not only can Member States be held responsible for infringements of Community law arising out of legislative and executive acts, but also out of judicial acts.[574] The Court confirmed the latter in 2003 in the case of *Gerhard Köbler*,[575] an Austrian university professor, who had been in employment with the University of Innsbruck under a public law contract. His contract with the university guaranteed him the wage of an ordinary university professor with a normal length-of-service increment.[576]

On that account Köbler put in an application to the responsible authorities in Austria, referring to the applicable national salary laws, requesting for a special length-of-service increment (SLSI), which under Austrian law was granted exclusively to professors who satisfied certain criteria, *inter alia*, the requirement of having been employed for a minimum of 15 years in universities of Austria.[577] In the line of argumentation put forward by Köbler he upheld the view that in spite of the fact that he had been unsuccessful in fulfilling the length-of-service prerequisite with universities of Austria,[578] as he only had ten years of teaching experience in Austria, he satisfied the required service duration due to his employment as a professor in Germany.[579] Thus, he contended that the time throughout which he had carried out teaching positions in universities of other Member States should also be taken into account.[580]

However, the Austrian authorities were of the opinion that an employment that was carried out in universities of other Member States did not contribute to the period of service required for attaining the SLSI.[581] Upon being confronted with the refusal of his request by the authorities, Köbler brought proceedings against the *Verwaltungsgerichtshof* (Austrian Supreme Administrative Court) asserting

574 Cf. Van Dam, 2013, p. 44.
575 *Köbler* (fn 15).
576 Cf. Van Dam, 2013, p. 44; cf. Lowry, 2004, p. 107.
577 Cf. Beutler, 2009, p. 778; cf. Lowry, 2004, p. 107.
578 Cf. Lowry, 2004, p. 107.
579 Cf. Biondi & Farley, 2009, p. 67.
580 Cf. Beutler, 2009, p. 778.
581 Cf. Van Dam, 2013, p. 45.

that his right to freedom of movement for workers, conferred by Community law under Art. 39 TEC [*now Art. 45 TFEU*], had been infringed.[582]

In the following legal proceedings the *Verwaltungsgerichtshof* deemed it necessary to refer to the ECJ for a preliminary ruling, which was recorded at the Registry of the Court under case number C-382/97[583]. After some months, the Registrar of the Court asked if it was still necessary to maintain the preliminary request brought forward by the Austrian supreme court, taking into consideration that the Court already had, in the meanwhile, handed down a ruling in the similar case of *Schöning-Kougebetopoulou*[584], [585] where it determined that "previous periods of comparable employment completed in the public service of another Member State [must be taken into account]"[586].[587]

However, it was not known at the time that the offer by the registrar to renounce the request for a preliminary ruling was made in error due to the fact that the *Verwaltungsgericht* in his reference to the ECJ put forward an incorrect explanation of the SLSI.[588] Therefore, the Austrian supreme court, following the offer by the registrar, solicited the positions of the parties on the matter and consequently renounced its request, having first and foremost maintained that on a tentative view of the subject-matter of the question, on which the preliminary ruling was based, had been settled in a manner beneficial to Köbler.[589] Regardless of this assessment, the *Verwaltungsgerichtshof*, in the end, rejected the claim by Köbler on the basis that the SLSI was in fact not a part of salary, but rather a bonus for loyalty with the objective intended to incentivize university professors to stay in Austria.[590] What is more, it held the view (which was later disputed) that "a statutory loyalty bonus [of such kind] is recognised by the Court of Justice as justification for legislation conflicting with the prohibition on discrimination"[591].

As Köbler was unable to appeal against the decision of the *Verwaltungsgerichtshof* adjudicating at last instance, he instead initiated proceedings for damages against Austria before the *Landesgericht für Zivilrechtssachen* (Re-

---

582 Cf. Schütze, 2012, p. 403.
583 Case C-382/97 *Gerhard Köbler v. Bundesminister für Wissenschaft, Forschung und Kunst* [1998] (case withdrawn).
584 Case C-15/96 *Kalliope Schöning-Kougebetopoulou v. Freie und Hansestadt Hamburg (Schöning-Kougebetopoulou)* [1998] ECR I-47.
585 Cf. Beutler, 2009, p. 778.
586 *Schöning-Kougebetopoulou* (fn 584), para 28.
587 Cf. Beutler, 2009, p. 778.
588 Cf. *Köbler* (fn 15), para 11; cf. Lowry, 2004, p. 107.
589 Cf. Beutler, 2009, p. 778.
590 Cf. Van Dam, 2013, p. 45; cf. Beutler, 2009, p. 778; cf. Lowry, 2004, p. 107.
591 *Köbler* (fn 15), para 11.

gional Court for Civil Law Matters) in Vienna, which was a lower civil court adjudicating at first instance.[592] In the process of these civil actions, the domestic court decided to halt the proceedings and, in accordance with the preliminary ruling procedure, refer five questions to the Court. Essentially these questions, which were submitted by the regional court in Vienna, inquired if the principle of State liability for violations of Community law also covered wrongful decisions of the judiciary, and, if that was the case, in which place of jurisdiction such an action should be scrutinized and according to which requirements such liability should be established. Conclusively, the Austrian regional court inquired whether the actions of the *Verwaltungsgerichtshof* in the present circumstances gave rise to liability of the State.[593]

6.1.2 Judgment of the Court

In its judgment in *Köbler* the ECJ referred to its previous ruling in *Brasserie/Factortame III*[594] where it held that the principle of State liability for violations of Community law was applicable regardless which authority of the Member State committed the infringement.[595] Furthermore, it, repeating the opinion of AG Léger,[596] who put forward that generally it was in line with the principle of State unity of international law that judicial acts are unequivocally associated with the State,[597] observed that

> [i]n international law a State which incurs liability for breach of an international commitment is viewed as a single entity, irrespective of whether the breach which gave rise to the damage is attributable to the legislature, the judiciary or the executive.[598]

The Court went on to emphasize the pivotal role which national judiciaries have assumed in the protection of individual rights flowing from provisions of Community law and the aspect that the full effectiveness of these provisions would be impaired and the judicial protection they conferred weakened if Member States could not be held liable for violations of Community law ascribed by their courts.[599] In his opinion in *Köbler*, AG Léger expanded on the issue by submitting that it would develop into an insurmountable contradiction if it was possible for the Member States to *prima facie* evade each and any liability for the acts or

592 Cf. Schütze, 2012, p. 403.
593 Cf. Lowry, 2004, p. 107.
594 *Brasserie/Factortame III* (fn 11).
595 Cf. Lowry, 2004, p. 107.
596 Opinion of AG Léger in Case C-224/01 *Köbler v. Austria* [2003] ECR I-10239.
597 Cf. ibid, paras 45-47; cf. Davies, 2012, p. 595.
598 *Köbler* (fn 15), para 32.
599 Cf. Streinz, 2012, p. 159.

omissions of its supreme courts, when as a matter of fact it was those courts, which had the particular responsibility of employing and safeguarding adherence to Community law.[600] Besides, the ECJ drew attention to the fact that because a violation of Community law by courts adjudicating at last instance could ordinarily not be revoked, they were, as a consequence, obliged to refer to the Court for a preliminary ruling pursuant to Art. 234(3) TEC [*now Art. 267(3) TFEU*].[601]

6.1.2.1 Res Iudicata Argument

Subsequently, the ECJ scrutinized whether the principle of State liability when applied to erroneous decisions by the judiciary was inclined to cast doubt on the principle of *res judicata.*[602] The principle of *res judicata*[603] *pro ventate habetur* (a matter adjudicated is held to be true) emanated from Roman law and its existence was acknowledged both by all Member States and by the legal system of the Community.[604] Although, as was duly pointed out by Komárek, there was no completely consistent interpretation of *res judicata* in all the legal orders pertaining to civil law.[605] Nonetheless, the principle implied that a ruling of a court, through which a conflict had been settled, could not be disputed other than by remedial actions stipulated by the respective legal order. On that account, where all remedial actions have been ineffectual, it followed that such a ruling, laid down by a court, could no longer be contested by inception of the same kind of legal proceeding.[606]

In the present circumstances, the main question of the parties to the case was whether the introduction of such kind of liability would impair the principle of *res judicata* and as a result impinged on both the autonomy and power of the judicial system.[607] At this point the Court, referring to its earlier judgment in *Eco Swiss,*[608] affirmed the significance of the principle of *res judicata,*[609] however it

---

600 Cf. Opinion of AG Léger in *Köbler* (fn 596), para 70.
601 Cf. Streinz, 2012, p. 159.
602 Cf. Schütze, 2012, pp. 403-404.
603 For a detailed analysis of the principle of *res judicata*, see Groussot, X., & Minssen, T. (2007). Res judicata in the Court of Justice case-law. *European Constitutional Law Review, 3*(3), 385–417; for cases regarding the finality of decisions, see Joined Cases C-392/04 and C-422/04 i-*21 v. Germany (i-21)* [2006] ECR I-8559 and Case C-453/00 *Kühne & Heitz* [2004] ECR I-837; for administrative decisions, see Case C-119/05 *Italy v. Lucchini (Lucchini)* [2007] ECR I-6199; for judicial decisions, see Case C-234/04 *Kapferer v. Schlank & Schick (Kapferer)* [2006] ECR I-2585.
604 Cf. Opinion of AG Léger in *Köbler* (fn 596), para 96.
605 Cf. Komárek, 2012, p. 69.
606 Cf. Opinion of AG Léger in *Köbler* (fn 596), para 96.
607 Cf. Lowry, 2004, p. 108.
608 Case C-126/97 *Eco Swiss China Time v. Benetton International (Eco Swiss)* [1999] ECR I-3055.
609 Cf. *Köbler* (fn 15), para 38; cf. *Eco Swiss* (fn 608), para 46.

came to the conclusion that the *Francovich* principle would not amend the ruling of courts adjudicating at the last instance, but instead afford reparation for the erroneous, final decision.[610] It made clear that

> the principle of State liability inherent in the Community legal order [set out] reparation, but not revision of the judicial decision which was responsible for the damage.[611]

Therefore, the ECJ, in accordance with the traditional nature of State liability, which as a matter of fact represented a judicial relief of final choice, restricted the State liability principle to national judiciaries whose decision could no longer be contested.[612]

6.1.2.2 Judicial Independence

In terms of the question on judicial independence, the Court drew attention to the fact that providing a basis upon which, under specific prerequisites, a liability claim against the State for violations of Community law by the judiciary could be established, did not entail the legal effects of decisions of a court adjudicating at last instance to be put into question. In the view of the ECJ the judicial independence was not being encroached upon, purely because it was not the judge who was personally liable, but rather the Member State. Moreover, it opined that making judicial relief available for erroneous decisions of national courts adjudicating at last instance did as a matter of fact not lead to a diminution, but rather reaffirmed the authority of the respective court. Furthermore, it was up to the Member States themselves to determine the competent court of jurisdiction, which adjudicated on such claims of State liability arising from violations of Community law by final instance courts.[613] The Court once more made a reference to the opinion of the Advocate General which asserted that a large amount of Member States acknowledged the principle of liability for decisions of the judiciary, because for the most part it was a principle common to their legal traditions.[614] In closing and to further sustain its reasoning, it pointed to the ECHR, which authorized the ECtHR to prescribe a State to make reparation for damages in case of violation of the Convention by a highest court.[615]

---

610 Cf. Schütze, 2012, p. 404.
611 *Köbler* (fn 15), para 39.
612 Cf. *Köbler* (fn 15), para 53; cf. Schütze, 2012, p. 404.
613 Cf. Streinz, 2012, p. 159.
614 Cf. Van Dam, 2013, p. 45.
615 Cf. Streinz, 2012, p. 159.

6.1.2.3 Conditions for Liability

After having established that the principle of State liability could also be applied to breaches of last instance courts, the ECJ turned to address the substantive requirements, which, in such a case, were necessary to be fulfilled. It held that, as a matter of principle, the common 'trinity' of criteria[616] laid down in its *Brasserie/Factortame III* judgment would be applicable in *Köbler* as well.[617]

At this point it should be recalled that until *Köbler* the application of the criteria had been restricted to cases where Community law had been infringed either by executive or legislative authorities.[618] According to Biondi & Farley, the position held from the beginning by the Court in *Köbler* amounted to a clear support for the general applicability of the liability principle established under *Francovich*, however, subsequently the ECJ weakened its approach substantially by narrowing down the second *Brasserie* condition, which pertained to the seriousness of the infringement of Community law.[619]

In this respect, the Court emphasized strongly that a mere infringement of Community law would not be a sufficient criterion to consider a Member State legally responsible for wrongdoings of its judiciaries.[620] Rather, according to its reasoning, such a choice of remedy should only be actionable "in the *exceptional case* where the court has *manifestly infringed* the applicable law",[621] resulting from the "specific nature of the judicial function and to the legitimate requirements of legal certainty"[622]. Thus, the ECJ inaugurated a stricter limit in the event of infringement of Community law by the judiciary and made it more demanding for a litigant to hold the State accountable for loss inflicted by an erroneous court decision.[623]

It was quite remarkable that the Court referred to a manifest infringement. Until now it could be inferred from earlier jurisprudence of the ECJ that in cases where the legislative powers of the State were afforded with broad discretion on a level equal to institutions and bodies of the Community in putting into effect Community rules, liability only resulted when these national powers manifestly and gravely ignored the confines of their discretionary competences. However, in *Köbler*, the Court spoke exclusively of the necessity of a manifest, but not

---

616 For an in-depth analysis of the criteria, see chapter 4.2.2 Conditions for Incurring Liability, p. 43.
617 Cf. *Köbler* (fn 15), para 52; cf. Schütze, 2012, p. 404.
618 Cf. Beutler, 2009, p. 776.
619 Cf. Biondi & Farley, 2009, p. 68.
620 Cf. *Köbler* (fn 15), para 121; cf. Beutler, 2009, pp. 779-780.
621 *Köbler* (fn 15), para 53 (emphasis added).
622 Ibid.
623 Cf. Scherr, 2012, p. 570.

grave infringement. Nevertheless, it could not be derived from this apparent change in terminology that the liability for infringements by the judiciary was in any way susceptible to less strict requirements.[624]

On the contrary, Tridimas believed that the rationale for this terminological inconsistency was based on a different motive. He put forward that the expressions manifest and grave concerned cases in which the legislative and administrative authorities were endowed with broad discretion in carrying out their duties and powers. However, Tridimas concluded that in stark contrast to their legislative and administrative counterparts, courts were not afforded with any similar discretion, therefore it could be deduced that discretion was not a suitable benchmark for establishing liability for violations by the judiciary.[625]

Scherr gave another rationale for the introduction of the criterion of a manifest breach. According to her viewpoint, and contrary to the opinion held by AG Léger,[626] the principle of State liability for violations of last instance courts was not a principle common to the legal traditions of the Member States.[627] In fact, at the time only in a few countries, including Belgium and Spain, had the courts recognized State liability for all acts of the judiciary. Whereas in various other countries, such as, France and the Netherlands, this course of action when it came to judicial proceedings was constrained and did not extend to the substance of judgments.[628] Consequently, according to her, the ECJ in *Köbler*, by referring to the criterion of a manifest breach, brought into effect an expressly limited system of the principle of State liability for infringements of Community law by the judiciary.[629] On this point, Lenaerts elaborated that to foster the effectiveness of Community law, the Court strived to "[take] the pulse of the national legal systems, to find the best solution in the middle-line".[630]

Therefore, the key question, following this assessment, was which rules should be employed to assert the occurrence of a manifest infringement. On this matter the Court initially provided some basic recommendations:[631]

> [The] factors include, in particular, the degree of clarity and precision of the rule infringed, whether the infringement was intentional, whether the error of law was excusable or inexcusable, the position taken, where ap-

624 Cf. Tridimas, 2007, pp. 151-152.
625 Cf. ibid, p. 152.
626 Cf. Opinion of AG Léger in *Köbler* (fn 596), para 85.
627 Cf. Scherr, 2012, p. 570.
628 Cf. Granger, 2007, p. 167.
629 Cf. Scherr, 2012, p. 570.
630 Lenaerts, 2003, p. 906.
631 Cf. Beutler, 2009, p. 780.

> plicable, by a Community institution and non-compliance by the court in question with its obligation to make a reference for a preliminary ruling under the third paragraph of Article 234 EC.[632]

Finally, the ECJ held that these requirements did not prohibit national courts of the Member States to incur liability under more lenient requirements and, despite the fact that the foundation of liability of Member States for violation of Community law by final instance courts was established by relevant provisions of national law, those provisions had to be in line with the principles of effectiveness and equivalence.[633]

By laying down these requirements the Court essentially reconciled its liability assessment for acts of the judiciary with the liability assessment for acts of the legislative.[634] In the case of the former, national courts, due to the exceptional circumstances of liability for erroneous judicial conduct,[635] were authorized to adopt the requirements for establishing liability in an especially strict manner.[636] It thereby followed that the question whether or not the infringement satisfied the criterion of being manifest was, in principle, to be decided by the competent court under the rules of national jurisdiction.[637] However, Beutler drew attention to the fact that in these peculiar circumstances, the ECJ believed itself to be in possession of all the intrinsic details necessary for making the judgment.[638]

6.1.2.4 Assessment of the Court

Hence, in *Köbler*, the Court proceeded to scrutinize whether or not the *Verwaltungsgerichtshof* had carried out a sufficiently serious infringement. Referring to its previous case law,[639] it pronounced that itself was not competent, in accordance with Art. 234(1) TEC [*now Art. 267(1) TFEU*] to determine whether a provision of national law was reconcilable with the laws of the Community. The ECJ followed the argument put forward by Köbler that the Austrian supreme court had disregarded Art. 39 TEC by backing the decision of the authorities to

---

632 *Köbler* (fn 15), para 55.
633 Cf. Lowry, 2004, p. 108.
634 Cf. Schütze, 2012, p. 404.
635 Cf. ibid.
636 Cf. Davies, 2012, pp. 596-597.
637 Cf. Biondi & Farley, 2009, p. 68.
638 Cf. Beutler, 2009, p. 780.
639 See, e.g. Joined Cases C-332/92, C-333/92 and C-335/92 *Eurico Italia & Others v. Ente Nazionale Risi (Eurico Italia)* [1994] ECR I-711, para 19; Joined Cases C-149/91 and C-150/91 *Sanders Adour SNC and Guyomarc'h Orthez Nutrition Animale SA v. Directeur des Services Fiscaux des Pyrenées-Atlantiques (Sanders Adour)* [1992] ECR I-3899, para 10.

rule out periods of employment in a university in another Member State from being considered for determining employment benefits.[640]

In spite of these findings, the Court concluded in the present case that the conduct of the *Verwaltungsgerichtshof* did not amount to a manifest breach of Community law.[641] This assessment was established on two rationales. The first being that the ECJ pointed out that Community law did not specifically deal with the issue of whether a loyalty bonus could act as a legitimate justification for impairing the freedom of movement for workers. It drew attention to the fact that an answer to such an issue could neither be found in the jurisprudence of the Court nor could such an answer be deemed as self-evident.[642] The second being that the ECJ maintained that the omission of the *Verwaltungsgerichtshof* to refer the matter to the Court for a preliminary ruling did in fact not change that conclusion.[643]

In this context, the Court referred to its judgment in *CILFIT*,[644] where it held that domestic courts are not obliged to make a reference to the ECJ provided that the correct adjudication of the law of the Community is so evident as to leave no discretion for any reasonable doubt.[645] However, prior to *Köbler*, no last instance court had ever depended on this *acte éclairé* doctrine,[646] and therefore, in principle, had to make a reference to the Court.[647] Consequently, the ECJ found that, although the Austrian supreme court, under the circumstances at hand, was not within its rights to rely on the doctrine,[648] it was still entitled to not make a reference for a preliminary ruling,[649] because "the *Verwaltungsgerichtshof* no longer considered it necessary to refer that question of interpretation to the Court"[650]. The explanation for the decision of the Austrian supreme court to revoke its request for a preliminary ruling was its erroneous interpretation of the ruling held by the ECJ in *Schöning-Kougebetopoulou*.[651]

---

640 Cf. Lowry, 2004, p. 108.
641 Cf. *Köbler* (fn 15), para 124; cf. Beutler, 2009, pp. 780-781.
642 Cf. *Köbler* (fn 15), paras 121-122; cf. Beutler, 2009, p. 781.
643 Cf. Tridimas, 2007, p. 153.
644 Case 283/81 *CILFIT v. Ministero della Sanità (CILFIT)* [1982] ECR 3415.
645 Cf. ibid, paras 3-4.
646 The *acte éclairé* doctrine was firstly established by the Court in Joined Cases 28-30/62 *Da Costa en Schaake NV & Others v. Nederlandse Administratie der Belastingen (Da Costa)* [1963] ECR 31; for a more recent case, see Case C-495/03 *Intermodal Transports BV v. Staatssecretaris van Financiën (Intermodal Transports)* [2005] ECR I-8151.
647 Cf. Biondi & Farley, 2009, p. 176.
648 Cf. *Köbler* (fn 15), para 118.
649 Cf. Biondi & Farley, 2009, p. 176.
650 *Köbler* (fn 15), para 123.
651 Cf. *Köbler* (fn 15), para 123; cf. Tridimas, 2007, p. 153.

It shall be noted that contrary to the Court, AG Léger was less lenient. In his opinion the *Verwaltungsgerichtshof* had committed an inexcusable mistake in assuming that the length-of-service increment was warranted regardless of its indirect discriminatory nature.[652] Thus, it was debated that the ECJ could have established a manifest breach of Community law. Under these circumstances, it may be suggested that *Köbler* contained a red flag from the Court to the supreme courts of the Member States taking advantage of the *acte éclairé* doctrine.[653]

6.1.3 Concluding Observations

The case of *Köbler* prompted critical responses before the judgment of the ECJ in the observations of the Member States during the litigation, and instantly thereafter when the Court in closing laid down its adjudication. According to Scherr, the judgment was greeted with little enthusiasm in the academic world. She put forward that if anything, the ruling gave rise to quite bewildered responses in academic publications and resentment by lawyers in the Member States.[654] In addition Beutler signified that the ruling of the ECJ in *Köbler* was definitely met with mixed opinions, although coming in at both ends of the spectrum.[655]

For instance, Breuer entirely approved of the judgment, opining that a different decision would have been perceived wrongly and inevitably resulted in a large rush of litigation.[656] Holding a similar view, Tridimas referred to *Köbler* as a model case in which the Court made use of an issue to map out the limitations of a new doctrine, prevent the likelihood of its illicit exploitation, and weaken its impact. He felt that the judgment represented a gate to litigation, intending to convey a final stance and desiring to deter following legal proceedings.[657]

Assuming a more critical and opposite standpoint, Wattel, notably himself a member of *Hoge Raad* (Dutch Supreme Administrative Court), strongly opined,[658] *inter alia*, that the judgment of the ECJ in *Köbler* was "a source of legal uncertainty, procedural entanglements and even more arrears"[659] and would result in "an avalanche of claims".[660] In that context, he put forward that as a result of *Köbler* wronged individuals would flood lower national courts with

652 Cf. Opinion of AG Léger in *Köbler* (fn 596), para 170; cf. Tridimas, 2007, p. 153.
653 Cf. Groussot & Minssen, 2007, p. 394.
654 Cf. Scherr, 2012, p. 571.
655 Cf. Beutler, 2009, p. 781.
656 Cf. Breuer, 2004, p. 251.
657 Cf. Tridimas, 2012, p. 373.
658 Cf. Wattel, 2004, p. 179.
659 Ibid, p. 177.
660 Ibid, p. 180.

claims, contending that a judgment of a court adjudicating at final instance impinged on their Community rights, or at the very least, that this court erred in not referring the case to the Court in a request for a preliminary reference on the issue.[661]

Consequently, the judgment of the ECJ in *Köbler* not only gave rise to a variety of opinions, but according to Chalmers, Davies, & Monti, also led to debates about legal certainty and established judicial hierarchies,[662] which Nassimpian appropriately coined as "yielding legal fireworks".[663]

In conclusion, the view may be taken that *Köbler* introduced a new stage in State liability. The Court discarded the notion of the unconditional impunity of the State and acknowledged, in special cases, the liability of the State for acts of its judiciary, which, in a fully developed democracy, can exist in the same place with the independence of the judicial authorities as well as the separations of powers.[664] By requiring specific conditions, the ECJ narrowed down the general obtainability of the remedy, as a result safeguarding the individual functions of both domestic and Community courts in the exercise of rights under the Community legal order. No such remedy should be afforded to claimants in situations where there still were alternative remedies available under national law, seeing as only domestic courts adjudicating at last instance were obliged to ask the Court for a resolution on an issue pertaining to Community law.[665] Thereby *Köbler* approved a right to damages, but no right to re-examination of a decision by a national court of last resort.[666] Thus, while taken into account its earlier jurisprudence, the ECJ issued in *Köbler*, as was generally understood, a principled and balanced judgment where it confirmed the validity of both the doctrine of primacy of Community law and the general applicability of remedies established under it.[667] To provide the reader with a better understanding of the judgment, it is outlined in Figure 4.[668]

However, while applying the principles developed by the *Köbler* jurisprudence, the following serious issue came to light: The Court had laid down that it was conceivable that Member States were held accountable for infringements of Community law by their final instance domestic courts. In addition, it had defined the prerequisites, which have to be fulfilled in this regard, and it had spe-

661 Cf. ibid.
662 Cf. Chalmers, Davies, & Monti, 2010, p. 310.
663 Nassimpian, 2007, p. 826.
664 Cf. Tridimas, 2007, pp. 158-159.
665 Cf. Lowry, 2004, p. 111.
666 Cf. Groussot & Minssen, 2007, p. 395.
667 Cf. Tridimas, 2007, pp. 158-159.
668 See Figure 4: The Köbler Judgment at a Glance, p. 98.

cifically stipulated a number of rules pertaining to the requisite of a manifest infringement. Nevertheless, as in the case of *Köbler* the infringement of Community law had ostensibly not been sufficiently serious enough, it continued to be undetermined at what stage the required limit would be achieved.[669] In other words, the matter on issue was if the prerequisite of a manifest infringement of Community law would turn out to be an overwhelming barrier.[670]

In *Commission v. Italy*,[671] just a few months after *Köbler*, the ECJ had to rule whether the *Corte Suprema di Cassazione* could be held accountable for an incorrect interpretation of the law of the Community. Advocate General Geelhoed in his opinion[672] in the case drew attention to the ruling of the Court in *Köbler* and consequently recommended to employ a set of criteria,[673] which he had laid down as part of his opinion, to determine whether or not an erroneous decision by a judiciary could lead to an infringement of Community law.[674] However, in his judgment, the Court, in the end, as pointed out by Dourado, settled on a different approach: The ECJ steered away from applying the *Köbler* doctrine by ultimately ruling that it was the Italian legislative, and not the judiciary in the first place, which was responsible for enacting tax laws that permitted national courts to eventually infringe Community law.[675]

In light of this, the prevailing opinion, advocated by legal authors including Türk, suggested that the *Köbler* remedy in practice was improbable to be successful.[676] Yet despite the fact that a claim for damages may have little probability of success, it still could be utilized as a measure to be given a decision by the Court that a national court adjudicating at final instance had infringed Community law.[677] In that regard, a State authority, confronted with the likelihood of reassessing a decision that infringed Community law, might have felt even less at ease with the doctrine in *Köbler* than with the one in *Brasserie/Factortame III* concerning the limitation of the scope of loss and damage. The opportunity to shed light on some of the unresolved issues, address reasonable concerns and expand on the requirements laid down in *Köbler* emerged in April of 2003.[678] It was in *Traghetti del Mediterraneo v. Italy*,[679] where the ECJ affirmed its judg-

---

669 Cf. Beutler, 2009, p. 782.
670 Cf. ibid.
671 Case C-129/00 *Commission v. Italy* [2003] ECR I-14637.
672 Opinion of AG Geelhoed in Case C-129/00 *Commission v. Italy* [2003] ECR I-14637.
673 Cf. ibid, paras 62-65.
674 Cf. Kaczorowska, 2013, pp. 386-387.
675 Cf. Dourado, 2008, p. 59.
676 Cf. Türk, 2009, p. 222.
677 Cf. Tridimas, 2007, p. 159.
678 Cf. Nassimpian, 2007, pp. 823-824.
679 Case C-173/03 *Traghetti del Mediterraneo SpA v. Italy (Traghetti)* [2006] ECR I-5177.

ment in *Köbler* by disapproving the legislation of Italy, which desired to considerably limit liability of the State for loss induced by a court adjudicating at last instance.[680]

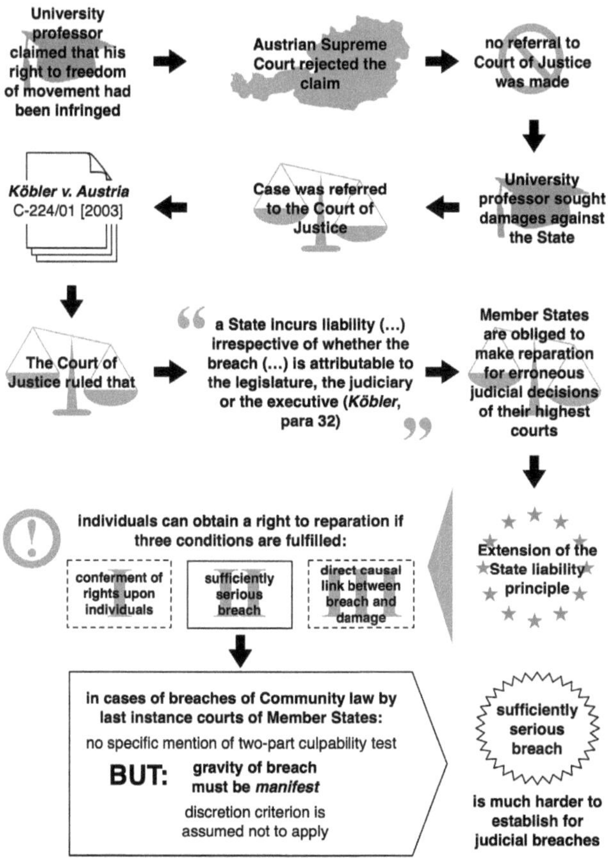

Figure 4: The Köbler Judgment at a Glance

Figure 4. The main aspects of the judgment in *Köbler* which expanded the principle of Member State Liability in damages by highlighting that it applied to breaches of Community law occasioned by the highest courts of Member States. In *Köbler* the key issue was whether an erroneous decision by a last instance court could trigger liability of the State. On that question the case referred to the Court of Justice which upheld the universality of the principle of State liability by holding it applicable in cases where last instance courts had erred in their decisions. The European Court, due to the special nature of the judiciary, strictly limited the right to reparation in such cases, by requiring the existence of a manifest infringement, making it more difficult for a claimant to incur liability of the State for wrongful decisions of final instance courts.

Source: Own compilation.

---

680 Cf. Craig & de Búrca, 2011, p. 246.

6.2 Affirmation of the Köbler Doctrine in Traghetti del Mediterraneo

6.2.1 Factual and Procedural Background

In the case, the claimant, Traghetti del Mediterraneo SpA (Traghetti SpA) had been a marine transport business, which, in the 1970s, conducted frequent transport services between mainland Italy and the islands of Sardinia and Sicily. In the beginning of the 1980s, Traghetti SpA, after enduring substantial losses, was compelled to dissolve its operation and initiated legal proceedings against a competitor by the name of Tirrenia di Navigazione (Tirrenia) in an attempt to obtain restitution for the loss that it argued to have sustained over several years as a consequence of fares being charged far below cost by Tirrenia.[681] Thus, Traghetti SpA contended that Tirrenia did not heed Italian competition laws and in addition violated Community law, especially by abusing its market dominance and being awarded public subsidies of doubtful legality.[682]

The *Tribunale di Napoli* (Naples District Court), a first instance court before which the claim was brought, rejected the lawsuit, and the successive appellate action before the *Corte d'appello di Napoli* (Naples Court of Appeal) was similarly rejected. Each court held that the subsidies had been legitimately awarded, since they were warranted by the general interest of the public in Southern Italy and did not have any harmful impact on the cross-sea traffic routes apart from, and contending with those opposed to by Traghetti SpA.[683]

Being of the opinion that the ruling of the Italian courts was founded on an erroneous reading of the Community laws on competition and State aid, and thus affected by errors of law,[684] Traghetti SpA made an appeal before the *Corte Suprema di Cassazione* (Italian Supreme Court of Cassation) and sought the Italian supreme court to make a reference to the European Court of Justice asking it for a preliminary ruling on the prevailing questions of interpretation of Community law.[685] However, the *Corte Suprema di Cassazione* upheld the ruling of the lower appellate court and refused to refer to the ECJ on the basis that the decision was in line with the jurisprudence of the Court as well as with the EC Treaty.[686]

681 Cf. Groussot & Minssen, 2007, p. 396.
682 Cf. Beutler, 2009, p. 783.
683 Cf. ibid.
684 Cf. Groussot & Minssen, 2007, p. 396.
685 Cf. Beutler, 2009, p. 783.
686 Cf. Albors-Llorens, 2007, p. 271.

Still, Traghetti SpA, taking the position that the Italian supreme court had erroneously construed the competition law provisions of the EC Treaty and that, as a court adjudicating at last instance, had in addition not complied with its obligation of reference under Art. 234(3) TEC, brought an action for damages against the Italian State before the *Tribunale di Genova* (District Court of Genoa). However, in the process there was one considerable obstacle:[687] The Italian legal system[688] ruled out any State liability for loss inflicted to individuals in which the violation was the outcome of an interpretation of legal rules, or of an analysis of the circumstances and evidence by that court. What is more, individuals were only permitted to make a claim for damages in the event of malice or gross negligence by the national court. On that account, Traghetti SpA put forward that these requirements were so strict that they made it extremely arduous, in fact effectively unattainable, to accomplish restitution from the State for loss inflicted by decisions of the judiciary.[689]

Since the *Tribunale di Genova* was not certain how to settle the case, it halted the legal process and made a reference to the ECJ for a preliminary ruling and sought clarification on the issue by referring two questions. As a result of the ruling in *Köbler*,[690] the Italian district court chose to take back the first question, as it had already been answered by the Court, but to keep the second question.[691] In light of compatibility of national legislation with Community law, the main question of the Italian court was whether national laws could either preclude or limit the State liability principle as laid down in the jurisprudence of the ECJ pertaining to the exercise of judicial powers.[692]

6.2.2 Judgment of the Court

Due to the extent of the question and in contrast to *Köbler*, the Court did not determine on its own if the *Corte Suprema di Cassazione* had carried out a manifest infringement of Community law.[693] It recalled the fundamental principles as laid down in *Köbler* while also making reference to its earlier jurisprudence.[694] It observed that for the principle of State liability under the EC Treaty, it made no difference which branch of government of a Member State had exercised its powers, and therefore, Member States could be held responsible for

687 Cf. ibid, pp. 271-272.
688 Cf. Art. 2(2) of Law No. 117 of 13 April 1988 on compensation for damage caused in the exercise of judicial functions and the civil liability of judges.
689 Cf. Biondi & Farley, 2009, p. 71.
690 Cf. *Köbler* (fn 15), paras 118-120.
691 Cf. Groussot & Minssen, 2007, pp. 396-397.
692 Cf. Albors-Llorens, 2007, p. 272.
693 Cf. Beutler, 2009, p. 784.
694 Cf. *Köbler* (fn 15), paras 30 et seqq.

the acts of their judiciaries. This was emphasized by the concept of judicial protection of individual rights. The judicature was devised to provide the safeguarding of rights flowing from Community law, and courts adjudicating at last instance are, as a matter of fact, the final judicial body to attain this protection.[695] In consequence, if the application of State liability for illegitimate acts of courts adjudicating at last instance were to be ruled out, then this would impinge on both general principles of effectiveness and effective judicial protection of Community law.[696]

Nevertheless, the ECJ did not turn a blind eye to arguments at odds with liability of such kind,[697] which were enshrined in the specific nature of the judiciary and the legitimate requirements of legal certainty.[698] Heeding the importance of these aspects previously recognized in *Köbler*, it restated that State liability in cases pertaining to the infringement of Community law by erroneous judicial acts was, in fact, "not unlimited"[699] and could give rise to liability only in cases that were exceptional in nature by establishing a manifest infringement.[700]

Ruffert put forward the view that this line of reasoning by the Court could not be seen as a novelty. However, according to him, what was novel in *Traghetti* was that the ECJ employed its course of reasoning in the appraisal of restrictions under national law to the liability inflicted by acts of the judiciary. The Court, while traditionally acknowledging the distinct role of courts in the resolution of conflicts, drew attention to the significance of the exercise of the act of interpretation of Community law, since it was undeniably possible that a domestic court could misread either substantive or procedural law of the Community.[701] As a result, an explicit denial of damages claims in such matters would be "tantamount to rendering meaningless the principle laid down by the ECJ in the *Köbler* judgment"[702]. This is even more to the point in the event of courts adjudicating at last instance, which are in charge of assuring the consistent interpretation of law in national legal systems.[703]

Furthermore, the Court adopted a similar approach in respect to the exclusion of infringements arising from the assessment of facts and evidence.[704] It ob-

695 Cf. Ruffert, 2007, p. 482.
696 Cf. Anagnostaras, 2006, p. 738.
697 Cf. Ruffert, 2007, p. 483.
698 Cf. *Köbler* (fn 15), para 32.
699 Ibid.
700 Cf. Nassimpian, 2007, p. 825.
701 Cf. Ruffert, 2007, p. 483.
702 *Traghetti* (fn 679), para 36.
703 Cf. Anagnostaras, 2006, p. 738.
704 Cf. Beutler, 2009, p. 785.

served that the minimum level necessary for establishing liability could also be met in the case of a domestic court carrying out an incorrect assessment of facts and evidence. Despite the fact that final instance courts, in principle, conducted interpretation of law rather than of fact, they, nonetheless, had to validate the categorization of facts and make sure that the rules of evidence were complied with. In the exercise of these duties, a manifest infringement of rules could evidently occur.[705] Concurring with the reflections of the Advocate General,[706] the ECJ highlighted that it would "amount to depriving the principle set out in the *Köbler* judgment of all practical effect"[707] if under such circumstances individuals would be excluded from holding a Member State responsible for violations of Community law. Referring to the circumstances in *Traghetti*, the Court pronounced that this was even more to be true for cases pertaining to State aid, where the safeguarding of rights which individuals "derive from Community law depends, to a great extent, on successive operations of legal classification of the facts"[708].[709]

Finally, in order to address all questions posed by the *Tribunale di Genova*, the ECJ held that State liability for breaches of the judiciary must neither be excluded, nor be constrained to cases of intent or gross negligence of the judge by national law, as such would impinge on the full effectiveness of Community law.[710] It held in clear terms that "under no circumstances may such criteria impose requirements stricter than that of a *manifest infringement* of the applicable law, as set out in paragraphs 53 to 56 of the *Köbler* judgment"[711]. Notably, even after the judgment in *Traghetti* the *Corte Suprema di Cassazione* proceeded to abide to the more stringent Italian scheme and the Italian State, consequently, in *Commission v. Italy*[712] was held to be repeatedly in violation of Union law.[713]

6.2.3 Concluding observations

The ruling of the Court in *Traghetti* adopted an identical approach to that applied in earlier jurisprudence of the ECJ for other types of State liability. As soon as it had been laid down that Member States could be held responsible for damages in case their supreme courts delivered or approved a manifestly incor-

---

705 Cf. Albors-Llorens, 2007, p. 272.
706 Cf. Opinion of AG Léger in Case C-173/03 *Traghetti del Mediterraneo SpA v. Italy* [2006] ECR I-5177, paras 49-89.
707 *Traghetti* (fn 679), para 40.
708 Ibid, para 41.
709 Cf. Beutler, 2009, p. 785.
710 Cf. *Traghetti* (fn 679), para 46; cf. Streinz, 2012, p. 159.
711 *Traghetti* (fn 679), para 44 (emphasis added).
712 Case C-379/10 *Commission v. Italy*, judgment of 2 November 2011, nyr.
713 Cf. Edward & Lane, 2013, p. 324.

rect assessment of Community rules, the principle of effectiveness would overcome any national rule that conflicted its stipulations.[714] Thereby, the ruling undeniably upheld the principle of supremacy of Community law. If national rules were to amend or restrict on purpose the principle of liability of the State or its fundamental requirements, then the consistent enforcement of Community law in this ambit would promptly be brought to naught.[715]

Consequently, *Traghetti* affirmed and elucidated the principles that were laid down in the earlier ruling of *Köbler*. The ruling illustrated that any restrictions, which were framed for State liability in the event of violations of Community law by final instance courts could not be construed in a way that would render State liability practically unattainable.[716] It followed that the national legal system was prevented to preclude liability for breaches of the judiciary pertaining to erroneous interpretation of rules and the incorrect appraisal of facts and evidence. Furthermore it was barred from setting up a criterion of liability exceeding the condition of manifest infringement established by jurisprudence of the Court. By advocating that claims in damages could only be established in situations where national courts of last resort have infringed Community law, the ruling also paid regard to the principle of *res judicata* and was in accordance with the principle of national procedural autonomy. In the light of effective restitution, the definition of a court of last resort had to be construed broadly as to include any adjudicating body against the decision of which there was no appellate remedy left.[717] In its ruling the ECJ avoided going into detail on the kinds of infringement which will be regarded manifest enough to make a damages claim possible.[718] While the Court had pronounced the significance of the lack of referral to the ECJ for a preliminary ruling, it remained rather opaque under which circumstances this would actually lead to a manifest infringement of Community law.[719]

As much as *Traghetti* exemplified that the Court gave special importance to the choice of words for framing the conditions of liability flowing from Community law, when it came to putting these rules into effect, it was inclined to deemphasize these very conditions, by that means making these provisions, largely, a form without substance. In the opinion held by Van Dam the doctrine laid down in *Köbler* was presumably the least substantial compared to the pro-

714 Cf. Anagnostaras, 2006, p. 746.
715 Cf. Albors-Llorens, 2012, p. 272.
716 Cf. Groussot & Minssen, 2007, pp. 398-399.
717 Cf. Anagnostaras, 2006, p. 746.
718 Cf. ibid.
719 Cf. Nassimpian, 2007, p. 826.

visions pertaining to the liability of the Member States for executive or legislative activities.[720]

Indeed, in light of jurisprudence of the ECJ up to this point it was striking that the Court, in cases such as *Köbler*, *Commission v. Italy*, and *Traghetti*, had not yet made any definite assertion pronouncing a supreme court liable for its non-compliance with Community law. However, this was about to change; it was in *Commission v. Spain*,[721] when the ECJ first ruled that a Member State had infringed Community law as a result of a decision by a court adjudicating at last instance.[722] In light of the above, it could be generally deduced that the principle of State liability pertaining to unlawful acts of the judiciary contributed only little to the existing system of effective judicial protection of individuals. The actual significance of the existence of such a liability principle perhaps was the likelihood to exert some influence over domestic courts adjudicating at last instance to conform to their obligations under Community law.[723] Therefore, it can be concluded that, the Court had, once again, not only interpreted the principle of State liability as a framework to safeguard the rights of individuals, but also as an implicit measure of last resort to ensure that the Member States observed their obligations under Community law.[724]

[720] Cf. Van Dam, 2013, p. 46.
[721] Case C-154/08 *Commission v. Spain* [2009] ECR I-187.
[722] Cf. Kaczorowska, 2013, p. 387.
[723] Cf. Anagnostaras, 2006, p. 747.
[724] Cf. Albors-Llorens, 2012, p. 273.

7 Liability of Individuals for Breach of European Law

The concept of State liability is applicable, as may be quite evident, where the State is responsible for an infringement of European law.[725] As already established by now, it was *ab initio* enshrined by the Court in *Francovich*,[726] where it held that the principle of State liability was "inherent in the system of the Treaty",[727] and could be applied pertaining to acts or omissions of any institution of the State.[728] This vertical scope of the principle of liability had long been restated, confirmed, and refined by jurisprudence[729] of the ECJ,[730] as a consequence establishing that one single legal framework dealt with all kinds of actions performed by "administrations and governments, local authorities, public bodies, legislatures, and even judiciaries"[731].[732] By contrast a horizontal scope of the principle had so far received little attention.[733]

However, in past years sizable interest arose over the possibility that the Court might introduce a private *Francovich* in its case law, that is a right to damages, flowing from the Treaty, pertaining to private law violations of obligations with direct effect under EC law.[734] Whereas general principles of Community law such as the principles of effectiveness and equivalence made it imperative that violations of EC rules by individuals be sufficiently indemnified through remedial provisions of national law, it was far from being clear-cut if there was a remedy of Community law available pursuant to which private parties would be held responsible to provide for the damage and loss sustained by other private entities. Yet, right from its very outset the legal order of the Community had planned that its rules could directly place duties on private parties. The question which now came into being was whether this also signified that an omission to carry out these obligations could induce a subordinate obligation to provide indemnification for damages sustained by other individuals.[735]

Subsequently, the ECJ carried out the assessment of this matter in *Courage Ltd v. Bernard Crehan*,[736] where, according to Van Dam, a new phase of develop-

725 Cf. Schütze, 2012, p. 405.
726 *Francovich* (fn 1).
727 Ibid, para 35.
728 Cf. *Brasserie/Factortame III* (fn 11), para 32.
729 See, e.g. cases *Traghetti* (fn 679); *Köbler* (fn 15); *Haim II* (fn 412); *Konle* (fn 547); *Brasserie/Factortame III* (fn 11).
730 Cf. Schütze, 2012, p. 405.
731 Granger, 2007, p. 159.
732 Cf. ibid, p. 159.
733 Cf. Schütze, 2012, p. 405.
734 Cf. Dougan, 2011, p. 430.
735 Cf. Schütze, 2012, p. 405.
736 Case C-453/99 *Courage Ltd v. Bernard Crehan (Courage)* [2001] ECR I-6297.

ment pertaining to the principle of liability had been achieved. It was in that case, where the Court debated the prospect of liability of private individuals and undertakings for an infringement of Community law, expressly for violation of competition law, namely Art. 81 TEC [*now Art. 101 TFEU*].[737] However, already some time before the significant ruling of the ECJ in *Courage*, there was arguable authority, initially put forward by AG Van Gerven in his opinion in the case of *Banks v. British Coal,*[738] that non-contractual liability, as a well-established general principle emanating from the Treaty, could easily be widened across, and geared to the needs of, any sort of non-contractual liability, including both cases of public and private law, therefore notwithstanding the fact whether they were vertical or horizontal in nature.[739]

7.1 The Banks Situation

All the issues up to this point have been associated with the jurisprudence of the Court concerning the principle of liability of Member States as well as bodies and institutions of the Community. Yet, in 1992, the English High Court referred to the ECJ in *Banks v. British Coal*[740] several inquiries regarding the interpretation basically of the antitrust provisions of the ECSC Treaty, Articles 65 and 66, as well as those of the correlating provisions of the EEC Treaty, Articles 85 and 86 [*ex Arts. 81-82 TEC; now Arts. 101-102 TFEU*]. One inquiry among many by the English High Court was whether domestic courts of the Member States have the authority, or in fact the duty, under Community law to provide reparation for the purpose of compensating loss or damage which private parties have sustained as a result of a breach of the abovementioned provisions on behalf of other private parties.[741]

In his opinion, AG Van Gerven had scrutinized the *Francovich* doctrine and perceived it as an *ius commune*, a common European law, flowing from the general system of the EC Treaty and its general principles and consequently, in striving for effective safeguarding of Community law rights against defendants emanating from both public and private areas, he gave preference to its applicability to breaches caused by private individuals.[742] The Advocate General strongly opined that:

[737] Cf. Van Dam, 2013, p. 47.
[738] Opinion of AG Van Gerven in Case C-128/92 *Banks v. British Coal (Banks)* [1994] ECR I-1209.
[739] Cf. ibid, paras 49-50; cf. Dougan, 2004b, p. 252.
[740] Case C-128/92 *Banks v. British Coal (Banks)* [1994] ECR I-1209.
[741] Cf. Van Gerven, 1996, p. 530.
[742] Cf. Weatherill, 2010, p. 512.

> The general basis established by the Court in the *Francovich* judgment for State liability also applies where an individual infringes a provision of Community law to which he is subject, thereby causing loss and damage to another individual. The situation then falls within the terms stated by the Court (...) of the *Francovich* judgment (and even earlier in *Van Gend en Loos*[743]), namely breach of a right which an individual derives from an obligation imposed by Community law on another individual.[744]

However, the ECJ had none of it, it did not follow the opinion of the Advocate General and, in what was to be a relatively short judgment, ruled that the respective provisions of the ECSC Treaty, quite contrary to the corresponding parts of the EC Treaty, were not directly effective, and moreover, that in default of a Commission decision establishing a violation on behalf of the defendants, Art. 65 ECSC did not confer any rights which domestic courts of the Member States must safeguard.[745] As regards to violations of Arts. 85 and 86 EEC, whose direct effect had already been established, the Court, in what according to Weatherill was a "cautious ruling carefully confined to the Coal and Steel Treaty",[746] avoided to rule on the matter in its entirety. Subsequently, it briefly touched upon the issue in *Brasserie/Factortame III*[747] when it observed in particular that State liability emerged in the case of violations of directly effective provisions of Community law,[748] and that "the right to reparation is the necessary corollary of the direct effect of the Community provision whose breach caused the damage sustained"[749]. But, it should take some more years before the ECJ was to directly manifest its bearing on the availability of reparation for violation of provisions of European competition law.[750]

7.2 The Courage Doctrine

Indeed, the present issue again came into existence in the competition law case of *Courage*, where the Court observed that a private party could be held responsible if it caused damage or loss by violating a provision of European law.[751] In fact, reparation must, generally, be obtainable to those who have sustained damage or loss as a result of an infringement of Arts. 81 or 82 TEC.

743 *Van Gend en Loos* (fn 5).
744 Opinion of AG Van Gerven in *Banks* (fn 738), para 43.
745 Cf. Van Gerven, 1996, p. 530.
746 Weatherill, 2010, p. 512.
747 *Brasserie/Factortame III* (fn 11).
748 Cf. Van Gerven, 1996, p. 530.
749 *Brasserie/Factortame III* (fn 11), para 22.
750 Cf. Weatherill, 2010, p. 512.
751 Cf. Van Dam, 2013, p. 47.

However, it is interesting to note that neither did the ECJ base its judgment on, nor did it expand upon the principle of State liability established in *Francovich* and *Brassier/Factortame III*.[752]

The case concerned a company with the name of Inntrepreneur Estates Ltd (IEL) which was established in 1990 through joint ownership by two companies, Courage Ltd, a brewery, and Grand Metropolitan plc, providing catering and hotel services, to consolidate their leased public houses. An arrangement made between IEL and Courage Ltd presupposed that all leaseholders of IEL were obliged to purchase their beer solely from Courage Ltd.[753]

In 1991, Bernard Crehan entered into two leasing contracts of public houses with IEL. Each of the leasing contracts had a duration of 20 years.[754] The exclusive purchase commitment (beer tie) clause of the lease contract could not be negotiated and consequently Crehan was obliged to buy a predefined minimum amount of varied beers at the leased public houses according to prices given in a price list maintained by Courage Ltd.[755] However, Crehan was in default of this contractual obligation and as a result the brewers brought an action for the recovery of the amount of £15,266 against him, which was presumed to be the total value of beers not paid that had been shipped to him.[756] In his defense the defendant challenged the exclusive beer purchasing commitment by claiming that it was illegal and therefore void, because it was contrary to Art. 81 TEC and in turn made a counter-claim by asking for compensation for the loss sustained out of the unlawful contract.[757]

Consequently, the legal proceedings centered around the question whether or not the conducted beer ties and leasing agreements were compatible with the competition law of the EC Treaty, and whether such compatibility or incompatibility had any bearing on the claims and counter-claims pursued by the parties to the litigation.[758] Crehan, it shall be brought to mind, was not just any third person affected in the cause of an anti-competitive business practice, but was himself part of a contract which was liable to be contested, because it conceivably led to an infringement of Art. 81 TEC. Against this background the English courts were disposed to perceive him as a member contributing to an anti-

752 Cf. Jones & Sufrin, 2008, p. 1331.
753 Cf. *Courage* (fn 736), para 3.
754 Cf. Jones & Sufrin, 2008, p. 1326.
755 Cf. Van Dam, 2013, p. 47.
756 Cf. Jones & Sufrin, 2008, p. 1326.
757 Cf. Schütze, 2012, p. 405.
758 Cf. Jones & Sufrin, 2008, p. 1326.

competitive act, but not as an aggrieved party in the proceedings.[759] Based on what is deemed the illegality principle, English courts adjudicating national law have in principle denied support to plaintiffs whose lawsuits were based upon unlawful acts, as well as to authorize parties to an illegitimate contract either to fulfill that agreement or to initiate any other legal action established upon it.[760]

However, the English court of appeal identified that a plausible interpretation of the law could be made in support of entitling a party to an illegitimate contract with the right to make a claim for reparation. It also approved of the reasoning, which was in support that said party was afforded rights by Art. 81 TEC, which were safeguarded by the law of the Community. It followed that if Crehan was not entitled to remedial action conveyed by English law then it would be conceivable that the provisions of English law refusing that privilege were not reconcilable, and had to be surrogated, with Community law. In that regard Community law, in particular Art. 81 TEC, might oblige the national court to provide rights, even in the case of a party that concluded an illegitimate contract, and adjudicate restitution for damage and loss sustained. The English court, confronted with these issues, made a preliminary reference to the European Court of Justice asking it for further guidance.[761]

The Court reasoned that the matter derived from the automatic invalidity rule in Art. 81(2) TEC [*now Art. 101(2) TFEU*], which was previously laid down by the ECJ in *Eco Swiss*[762]. It went on to declare "that any agreements or decisions prohibited pursuant to that article are to be automatically void"[763]. Moreover, it put forward that, because the article was directly effective, any single person, in spite of being a contracting party that was responsible to constrain or distort competition under Art. 81(2) TEC, could depend upon the violation of that rule before a domestic court of a Member State. As it is the duty of the domestic courts of the Member States to effectively safeguard the rights conveyed upon individuals by virtue of European law, such a party was generally entitled to make a claim for restitution for damages sustained out of the contract.[764] The Court observed:

> The full effectiveness of Article [81] of the Treaty and, in particular, the practical effect of the prohibition laid down in Article [81(2)] would be put at risk if it was not open to any individual *to claim damages for loss*

[759] Cf. Weatherill, 2010, p. 512.
[760] Cf. Jones & Sufrin, 2008, p. 1326.
[761] Cf. ibid, p. 1328.
[762] *Eco Swiss* (fn 608).
[763] *Courage* (fn 736), para 21; see also *Eco Swiss* (fn 608), para 36.
[764] Cf. Van Dam, 2013, pp. 47-48.

> *caused to him by a contract or by conduct liable to restrict or distort competition.* Indeed, the existence of such a right strengthens the working of the Community competition rules and discourages agreements or practices, which are frequently covert, which are liable to restrict or distort competition. From that point of view, actions for damages before the national courts can make a significant contribution to the maintenance of effective competition in the Community.[765]

After putting an emphasis on the significance of private enforcement of Community law, the ECJ went on to observe that an action in damages must not be conditionally barred, despite a case where it is being made by an individual who himself is a party in a contract that infringes competition law. As the principle of illegality under English law precluded such an unrestricted approach to action in damages, it held that it would be deemed incompatible with Community law.[766]

However, the Court also established that, with regard to the general principle that a claimant must not profit from his own illegitimate course of action,[767] Community law, generally, did not preclude domestic law from disallowing the right to obtain damages to an individual who was adjudged to "bear significant responsibility for the distortion of competition"[768].[769] In that respect, national courts, firstly had to established whether or not the claimant would profit out of the situation, a variety of factors had to be regarded, *inter alia*, if one contracting party was significantly more powerful than the other and as a result could exert an oppressive influence over the other by enforcing less favorable terms and conditions upon it,[770] and secondly, had to make sure that the principles of effectiveness and equivalence of Community law were followed.[771]

In this context, Albors-Llorens argued that it was arduous to establish in which ways the principle of illegality could be irreconcilable with Community law. According to her, an impediment to claims for reparation sought by a party to an unlawful contract was both part of a number of domestic legal orders of the Member States and appeared to be a consistent emanation of the principle of estoppel.[772] However, the crucial point was that the aforementioned principle of national law had been formulated so universally that it seriously encroached

765 *Courage* (fn 736), paras 26-27 (emphasis added).
766 Cf. Jones & Sufrin, 2008, p. 1333.
767 Cf. *Slaughtered Cows* (fn 84), para 10.
768 *Courage* (fn 736), para 31.
769 Cf. Van Dam, 2013, p. 48.
770 Cf. ibid.
771 Cf. *Courage* (fn 736), para 29.
772 Cf. Albors-Llorens, 2002, p. 39.

upon the effectiveness of Community law.[773] In closing Albors-Llorens pointed out that this was, in fact, not a totally novel occasion, because as it could be observed in *Rewe*,[774] *Factortame I*,[775] and *Marshall II*,[776] the jurisprudence of the ECJ on domestic remedial action for violations of Community law had always suffered from the conflict between the two inherently contrasting principles of effectiveness and procedural autonomy.[777]

Regarding the right to damages, the Court in *Courage* did not *expressis verbis* refer to it as it had done earlier in the cases of *Francovich* and *Brasserie/Factortame III*, however, its ruling still determined that Art. 81 TEC conveyed rights upon private parties, even in the event of a breach of contract, and that any violation of the article was sufficiently serious to obtain a right to make a damage claim by virtue of Community law. Thus, private parties must be afforded with the right to bring action for damages for any loss sustained out of a contract or demeanor which constrained competition. Jones & Sufrin were of the opinion that these circumstances gave reason to believe that in the event of a violation of competition law, there was a default presumption that the first two requirements of *Brasserie/Factortame III* were satisfied. Nevertheless, the ECJ in *Courage*, in stark contrast to *Brasserie/Factortame III*, did not expressly require that there must be a direct causation between the violation of the duty by the accused person and the loss suffered by the aggrieved party. This gap had to be filled by provisions of national law on causation.[778]

Unfortunately, the silence of the Court on these matters created an obvious lacuna in its line of argumentation. While it decisively pointed to national law for detailed procedural rules, it did not bring up the particularities of substantive law at all, only speaking of the availability of the right itself, which was held to be emanating from Art. 81 TEC.[779] Schütze exemplified the gap in the reasoning of the ECJ on the basis of several issues that were left unresolved. He submitted that it did not flow from the judgment of the Court whether the newly founded *Courage* doctrine constituted a European or national remedy, nor whether it was an extension of the *Francovich* doctrine to private parties or a self-standing regime of liability.[780] The same view was shared by Craig & de Búrca, who were

---

[773] Cf. Opinion of AG Mischo in Case C-453/99 *Courage Ltd v. Bernard Crehan* [2001] ECR I-6297, para 52; cf. Albors-Llorens, 2002, p. 39.
[774] *Rewe* (fn 115).
[775] *Factortame I* (fn 135).
[776] Case C-271/91 *Marshall v. Southampton and South West Hampshire Area Health Authority (Marshall II)* [1993] ECR I-4367.
[777] Cf. Albors-Llorens, 2002, pp. 39-40.
[778] Cf. Jones & Sufrin, 2008, pp. 1333-1334.
[779] Cf. Basedow, 2007, pp. 237-238.
[780] Cf. Schütze, 2012, p. 406.

of the opinion that the obligation of national courts to make available an action for damages against a private party for a violation of other Treaty rules beyond competition rested unclear.[781] Schütze also put forward the subtle opinion that the "original ambivalence surrounding the principle of State liability"[782] from that time onward also encompassed the principle of private liability established in *Courage*.[783]

Indeed, it was these ambiguities which as a consequence led to divergent readings being handed down for identical circumstances by national courts of the Member States. For example, the wording of the ruling of the ECJ in *Courage*, speaking that Art. 81(1) TEC [*now Art. 101(1) TFEU*] conferred rights upon "any individual",[784] was kept vague enough to allow for both contractual and non-contractual claims to be brought before national courts. However, in the ambit of claims made by parties to the contract under the article, it was not clear-cut whether those rights had to be afforded to both competing undertakings and consumers.[785] Nonetheless, all these ambiguities that abided due to the line of thought, which the Court had chosen in *Courage*, were dissipated after its ruling in *Manfredi v. Lloyd Adriatico Assicurazioni*[786] in 2006,[787] which, according to Schütze, had a similar elucidatory effect as *Brasserie* after *Francovich*.[788]

Still, all lack of clarity aside, the ruling of the ECJ in *Courage*, according to Albors-Llorens, was "deeply progressive"[789]. It had to be understood as advocacy by the Court of the twofold motives of the competition legal regime established by the Commission. Firstly, it expressly endorsed the argument that claims for damages between parties to a contract could be utilized as worthwhile measures of public policy to foster competition, and secondly, it advocated the complete autonomous usage of Art. 81 TEC without any reservation.[790]

7.3 Manfredi as a Private Brasserie

In *Manfredi*, a private party by the name of Vincenzo Manfredi and others, who all were Italian consumers, filed lawsuits against their automotive insurance companies. Together they alleged that these businesses had been taken part in

781 Cf. Craig & de Búrca, 2011, pp. 246-247.
782 Schütze, 2012, p. 406.
783 Cf. ibid.
784 *Courage* (fn 736), para 26.
785 Cf. Drake, 2006, pp. 855-856.
786 Joined Cases C-295/04 and C-298/04 *Manfredi v. Lloyd Adriatico Assicurazioni & Others (Manfredi)* [2006] ECR I-6618.
787 Cf. Van Dam, 2013, p. 48.
788 Cf. Schütze, 2012, p. 406.
789 Albors-Llorens, 2002, p. 40.
790 Cf. ibid, p. 41.

anti-competitive practices, by a consequence of which the insurance premiums charged to them had been on average 20% higher than regular payments would have been, and consequently sought for compensation of damages.[791] In the present case, the ECJ not only affirmed its ruling in *Courage,*[792] but what was more pronounced that

> [i]t follows that *any individual* can claim compensation for the harm suffered where there is a causal relationship between that harm and an agreement or practice prohibited under Article 81 [of the] EC [Treaty].[793]

According to this, a violation of the competition provisions of the EC Treaty automatically qualified for liability, and no further establishment of fault was necessary.[794] Moreover, the Court contemplated how reparation should be determined and quantitatively calculated with regard to the principle of effectiveness. It ruled that aggrieved parties had to be afforded the right to make claims for damages not only for actual loss (*damnum emergens*), but also for loss of profit (*lucrum cessans*) to which is to be added interest.[795] In addition, it held that Art. 81 TEC did not preclude national courts from granting exemplary damages, exceeding the benefit received by the undertaking in violation of competition rules, as a result acting as a deterrent against the conclusion of unlawful arrangements.[796]

The ruling of the ECJ in *Manfredi* essentially laid down the scope of the right to damages for violation of Art. 81 TEC pertaining to, *inter alia*, inclusion of consumers as subjects of rights afforded under the article, existence of a causal relationship, periods of limitation and the quantum of damages obtainable. The Court attached great importance to retain consistency with the existing legal order of the Community by evolving these provisions, where it was realizable, concurrently with those pertaining to damages in other ambits of Community law.[797] However, the question came into being whether it could be rightfully assumed that post-*Courage* the ECJ had established an *ius commune* to damages between private parties under Art. 81 TEC, which had extensive ramifications in terms of expanding across the ambit of competition law of the Community.[798] In the view of Schütze, such interpretation might be established on the

---

791 Cf. Schütze, 2012, p. 406.
792 Cf. *Courage* (fn 736), para 26.
793 *Manfredi* (fn 786), para 61 (emphasis added).
794 Cf. Van Dam, 2013, p. 48.
795 Cf. *Manfredi* (fn 786), para 95; cf. Van Dam, 2013, p. 48.
796 Cf. *Manfredi* (fn 786), para 93; cf. Jones & Sufrin, 2008, p. 1334.
797 Cf. Drake, 2006, pp. 858.
798 Cf. ibid.

grounds of the "constitutional language and spirit of the ruling",[799] which the Court seemed to have adopted on the matter starting with *Courage*.[800]

7.4 Concluding Observations

While academic debate raged on trying to reach common accord on how to properly construe the advance of the ECJ into the policies of private liability to make good damages under the competition law of the Community, it became in any event evident that *Courage* neither expanded the liability principle laid down in *Francovich* to legal disputes between private legal persons, nor bring into line the conditions for establishing liability claims, firstly enshrined in *Francovich* and later restated and affirmed in *Brasserie/Factortame III*, so as to also apply to behavior of private parties.[801]

This conclusion, which suggested otherwise, was derived from the fact, held by the Court in *Manfredi*, that an action for damages could be pursued by merely establishing a causal connection between the damage sustained and the conduct not permitted under Community law, because it was evidently missing the requirement of a sufficient serious breach, the second criterion laid down by the ECJ in *Brasserie/Factortame III*.[802] By extension of this matter it could be concluded that the liability regime for private individuals and undertakings differed from that of Member States. In case of the latter a sufficiently serious violation of Community law was necessary, whereas for the former any violation of Community law, such as provisions of competition law, ought to be adequate.[803] The emergence of this argumentation resulted in a substantial weakening of the view that the sufficiently serious breach condition was a general principle, flowing from legal traditions common to the Member States, suitable for taking care of all breaches of Community law, both private and public, with the exception of the most highly abstracted cases.[804]

Schütze emphasized that this line of reasoning casted doubt, whether or not there indeed was a unified approach for non-contractual liability available for both public and private breaches of European law.[805] Consequently this meant that the *ius commune* approach to any kind of non-contractual liability, on which the academic debate centered on, was unable of unifying itself completely with the case law of the Court, whose reasoning of parallelism, that is the possibility

799 Schütze, 2012, p. 406.
800 Cf. ibid.
801 Cf. Dougan, 2004b, p. 254.
802 Cf. Schütze, 2012, p. 407.
803 Cf. Van Dam, 2013, p. 49.
804 Cf. Dougan, 2004b, p. 254.
805 Cf. Schütze, 2012, p. 407.

of choosing remedial action, either under *Francovich* or through other remedies flowing from Community law, would in any event confront some plaintiffs with different outcomes depending on which rights they based their claims on.[806]

In closing, it can be established on these grounds that, despite the rather aspiring theory put forward by AG Van Gerven in his opinion in *Banks*,[807] it seemed more realistic to assume that the liability principle under *Francovich* was indeed limited to the ambit of public law, while liabilities arising out of cases of private law, may they be vertical or horizontal in nature, continued to be examined through differing legal regimes of Community law.[808] The judgments of the ECJ, initially in *Manfredi*, and subsequently in *City Motors*,[809] have confirmed the fundamental availability of a right to reparation against private parties emanating from the legal order of the Community, to be used under determined circumstances, such as in the field of competition law.[810] Thus, it can be concluded, as illustrated in detail by Figure 5,[811] that the doctrine of private liability, established by the European Court in *Courage,* was applicable only where provisions of Community law expressly provided for damage actions between private parties in the event of a violation of obligations imposed on individuals, therefore constraining its applicability to a very limited field of Community legislation.[812]

---

806 Cf. Dougan, 2004b, p. 255.
807 See generally Opinion of AG Van Gerven in *Banks* (fn 738).
808 Cf. Dougan, 2004b, p. 255.
809 Cf. Case C-421/05 *City Motors Groep v. Citroën Belux (City Motors)* [2007] ECR I-653, para 33.
810 Cf. Dougan, 2011, p. 430.
811 See Figure 5: Comparison of the Courage Doctrine to the Principle of State Liability, p. 119.
812 Cf. Schütze, 2012, p. 407.

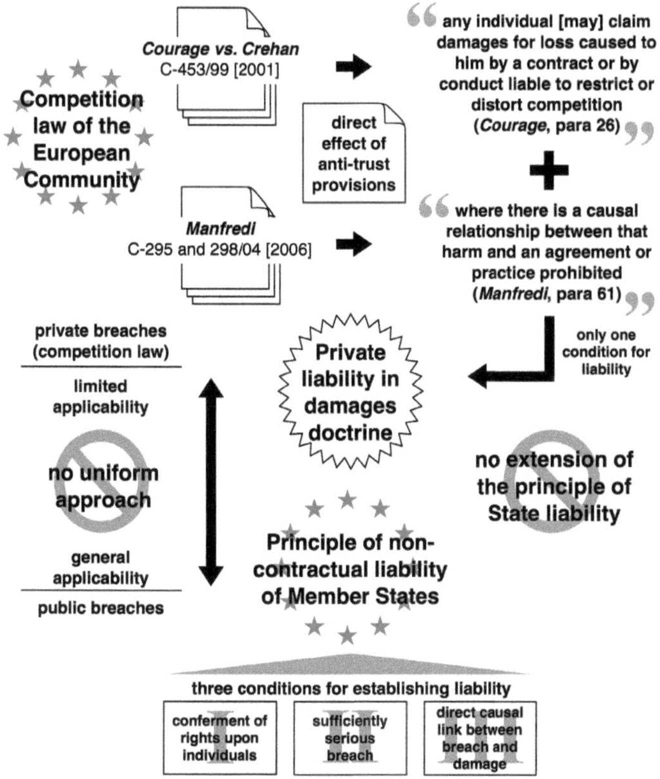

Figure 5: Comparison of the Courage Doctrine to the Principle of State Liability

Figure 5. The differences between the private liability in damages doctrine under *Courage* and the principle of State liability. The liability of private actors stems from the direct effect of the antitrust provisions of Community law. As the conditions to incur liability differ between the two regimes, no uniform approach can be established. Consequently, the *Courage* doctrine does not represent an extension to the principle of State liability. While the latter is a universal principle with general applicability, the former is limited to the ambit of competition law.

Source: Own compilation.

8 Conclusion

The purpose of this thesis was to inquire into the foundations, inauguration and development of the principle of Member State liability by analyzing the jurisprudence of the Court over time, as well as to afford the reader with a thorough grasp of the subject. Additionally, it sought to determine whether the existence of a fourth stage in the evolution of the principle could be demonstrated.

In the 1960s, prior to *Francovich*,[813] in a still nascent Community, the Court was primarily concerned with issues of enforcing Community law and its compliance by Member States. To secure these objectives, the ECJ placed reliance on the role of individuals in the enforcement of Community law by introducing the principle of direct effect. Yet, the remedial limits of the principle required an explicit right in damages to be established for breaches of Community law. As providing a legal basis for the existence for such a right in the legal order of the Community proved difficult, the Court, ultimately, acknowledged the non-contractual liability of the Member States without identifying its legal basis. In light of this, the ECJ held that Member States were liable for their breaches of Community rules because of their duty to afford effective protection of individual rights. However, as the Court avoided providing either a general definition of State liability or its requirements, a wronged individual seeking recovery of damages could only turn to national liability regimes, which were to a large extent divergent. As a consequence, the effectiveness of Community law was questionable, because the effective protection of individual rights was not guaranteed.

In 1991, to settle these issues, the Court had introduced the principle of State liability in *Francovich*. A group of Italian employees, who were owed back payments of wages by their insolvent employer, turned to the law to make claims on guarantees provided under Community law. However, as the directive was not transposed into Italian law, and did not have direct effect, their claims ended up having no legal basis. While placing reliance upon the general principles of effectiveness, judicial protection of individual rights and duty of loyal cooperation, the ECJ used this precedent to adjudge that Member States had an obligation "to make good loss and damage caused to individuals by breaches of Community law for which they can be held responsible".[814] Therefore, if a Member State failed to implement a directive, it could be held liable as long as three requirements were met: firstly, the provision in question must confer rights upon individuals, secondly, the right derived from the directive must be founded

813 *Francovich* (fn 1).
814 Ibid, para 37.

on its provisions, and thirdly, a causal link between the breach of Community rights by the State and the loss and damage sustained by the individual must exist. Although the judgment of the Court in *Francovich* founded the non-contractual liability of the Member States, it did so on very general terms so as not to encroach on the procedural autonomy of the Member States. Consequently, the ECJ was required to provide more indications as to the liability regime for breaches of Community law in cases that followed.

In 1996, the judgment in the joined cases of *Brasserie/Factortame III*,[815] by replacing the particular conditions for liability for the non-implementation of a directive with the conditions of conferral of rights, sufficiently serious breach and direct causal link, which were applicable to all violations of Community law, affirmed, clarified and extended the *Francovich* principle. Both cases concerned wrongful acts of national legislatures which were contrary to provisions of primary law of the Community and for which recovery of damages was not obtainable under applicable national laws. By holding the principle of State liability applicable in cases, where directly applicable provisions of the Community legal order were infringed and regardless of which authority of the Member State had incurred the damage, the Court made it a universal principle. To substantiate its ruling the ECJ referred to the non-contractual liability of the Community under which the Community was also liable for the wrongful behavior of its law making institutions. This reference enabled it to revise the second criterion of State liability by deploying the requirement that "the breach must be sufficiently serious",[816] which "implie[d] a manifest and grave disregard by the Member State for the limits set on its discretion".[817] Although, the Court subsequently gave guidelines in its judgment on how to gauge the legality of measures, in practice, the novel and sophisticated test ended up being byzantine, raising even more questions.

The case law after *Brasserie/Factortame III*, founded on preliminary rulings, primarily revolved around the clarification of the conditions for establishing State liability. The ECJ either gave guidance to national courts on how to properly interpret the conditions of liability or took an active part in determining itself whether or not they were fulfilled. In the former context, it revised the sufficiently serious breach criterion in the course of the case law, by initially applying a two-part test based on the gravity of the breach and the extent of the discretion af-

815 *Brasserie/Factortame III* (fn 11).
816 Ibid, para 51.
817 *Robins* (fn 433), para 70.

forded to the State authority,[818] but later on giving less importance to the element of discretion in favor of more objective conditions such as the "clarity and precision of the rule breached"[819] criterion.[820] The Court also observed that a breach was sufficiently serious if there had been a previous judgment or case law declaring an infringement in the matter.[821] In the latter context, it, from time to time, mostly in questions of policy, by using the conditions as overriding instruments, resorted to limit the right to State liability.[822] Sometimes the rulings of the ECJ were contradictory[823] or inconsistent.[824] Also, the Court deferred cases back to the national courts when there was no evident solution whether an infringement could be established.[825] Finally, the ECJ also scrutinized the compatibility of national rules in light of the principle of State liability. These rules, *inter alia*, set time limits,[826] delimited liability to State organs,[827] posed additional requirements,[828] or required a specific conduct of the claimant.[829] However, not all cases contributed to the further development of the jurisprudence of the Court in Member State liability. In many cases,[830] it remarked, by way of *obiter dictum*, that recovery of damages arising out of liability of the State was a legitimate legal remedy with little further explanation.

818 See, e.g. *Denkavit* (fn 391), para 50; *Dillenkofer* (fn 397), paras 25-26; *Hedley Lomas* (fn 394), paras 25, 28; *British Telecom* (fn 386), paras 39-40, 42; *Brasserie/Factortame III* (fn 11), para 45.

819 *Brasserie/Factortame III* (fn 11), para 56.

820 See, e.g. *Gervais Larsy* (fn 413), para 39; *Haim II* (fn 412), paras 41-43.

821 See, e.g. Case C-446/04 *Test Claimants in the FII Group Litigation v. Commissioners of Inland Revenue (FII Group)* [2006] ECR I-11753, paras 214-215; *Gervais Larsy* (fn 413), paras 43-44.

822 For limitation through the conferment of rights criterion, see *Ten Kate* (fn 494), paras 27-28; *Peter Paul* (fn 488), para 50; for limitation through the direct causal link criterion, see *Leth* (fn 467), paras 46-48; *Danfoss* (fn 460), para 39; *Brinkmann* (fn 445), para 29.

823 Contrast *Combinatie Spijker* (fn 502), paras 86-87 with *Stadt Graz* (fn 499), para 39.

824 Contrast *Danske Slagterier* (fn 504), paras 22, 24 with *Peter Paul* (fn 488), para 46.

825 See, e.g. *DEB* (fn 517), para 60; *Evans* (fn 514), paras 84-85.

826 See, e.g. *Palmisani* (fn 534).

827 See, e.g. *Haim II* (fn 412); *Konle* (fn 547).

828 See, e.g. *Fuß II* (fn 510); *AGM-COS.MET* (fn 430).

829 See, e.g. *Transportes Urbanos* (fn 568); *Stockholm Lindöpark* (fn 422); *Metallgesellschaft* (fn 566).

830 See, e.g. Case C-81/98 *Alcatel Austria AG & Others, Siemens AG Österreich and Sag-Schrack Anlagentechnik AG v. Bundesministerium für Wissenschaft und Verkehr (Alcatel Austria)* [1999] ECR I-7671, para 49; Case C-258/97 *Hospital Ingenieure Krankenhaustechnik Planungs-Gesellschaft mbH v. Landeskrankenanstalten-Betriebsgesellschaft (Hospital Ingenieure)* [1999] ECR I-1405, para 27; Case C-131/97 *Annalisa Carbonari & Others v. Università degli studi di Bologna, Ministero della Sanità, Ministero dell'Università e della Ricerca Scientifica and Ministero del Tesoro (Carbonari)* [1999] ECR I-1103, paras 51-52; Case C-111/97 *EvoBus Austria GmbH v. Niederösterreichische Verkehrsorganisations GmbH (Evobus)* [1998] I-5411, para 21; Case C-97/96 *Verband deutscher Daihatsu-Händler eV v. Daihatsu Deutschland GmbH (Daihatsu)* [1997] ECR I-6843, para 25; Case C-90/96 *David Petrie & Others v. Università degli studi di Verona and Camilla Bettoni (Petrie)* [1997] ECR I-6527, para 31; Case C-54/96 *Dorsch Consult Ingenieurgesellschaft mbH v. Bundesbaugesellschaft Berlin mbH (Dorsch Consult)* [1997] ECR I-4961, para 45; Joined Cases C-192/95 to C-218/95 *Comateb & Others v. Directeur General des Douanes et Droits Indirects (Comateb)* [1997] ECR I-165, para 34.

In 2003, the Court extended its *Francovich* and *Brasserie/Factortame III* case law in *Köbler*[831] by ruling that Member States could also be held liable for manifest infringements of Community law arising out of judicial acts by their highest courts. The case concerned an Austrian university professor who sought damages against the State after his request for a salary increment due to teaching positions held in Germany was ultimately turned down by one of the supreme courts of Austria. The ruling of the ECJ in *Köbler* was seminal and principled. The Court walked a tightrope between expanding the principle of State liability to judicial breaches, while safeguarding both the principles of national procedural autonomy and *res judicata*. On one side, it waived the unconditional immunity of the State and its organs, but on the other it strictly limited the general applicability of the principle of State liability by introducing the requisite of a manifest infringement, so that the effective functioning of national and Community courts was protected. However, compared to other principles, the introduction of the *Köbler* damages doctrine raised a lot of dissenting opinions as well as probing questions on how to establish whether a breach was sufficiently serious based on the new manifest infringement criterion for judicial breaches. Consequently, in the cases that followed the ECJ was neither inclined to apply the doctrine of *Köbler* nor to specify the circumstances leading to a manifest infringement of Community law. Instead, the Court, subsequently, sought ways of upholding its judgment in *Köbler*, and by resorting to the general principle of effectiveness, it affirmed the doctrine in *Traghetti del Mediterraneo*,[832] while on the same grounds ruling out any restrictions of the principle of State liability by national rules.

Until now, it had been established by case law that the principle of Member State liability had general applicability and therefore provided a unified approach to non-contractual liability of Member States for breaches of Community rights. The unified approach concerned wrongful acts and omissions of "administrations and governments, local authorities, public bodies, legislatures, and even judiciaries".[833] Consequently, the question was whether the principle could be adopted to apply to any kind of non-contractual liability, including private law situations, and possibly herald in a fourth stage in the evolution of State liability. In the cases of *Courage v. Crehan*[834] and *Manfredi*[835] the ECJ had occasion to concern itself with that eventuality. Both cases centered on the antitrust rules of competition law formulated in the Treaty. Although the Court held that due to

831 *Köbler* (fn 15).
832 *Traghetti* (fn 679).
833 Granger, 2007, p. 159.
834 *Courage* (fn 736).
835 *Manfredi* (fn 786).

the direct effect of the antitrust provisions, any party could rely upon violation on the provisions and consequently bring a claim for damages before national courts, it did not explicitly refer to a right to damages under Community law. As the ECJ in *Manfredi* furthermore only required a direct causal link to establish damages, it became evident that the cases neither extended the *Francovich* principle nor advanced its unified approach in establishing liability claims. Therefore the doctrine of private liability introduced in *Courage vs. Crehan* applied only in a very limited field of Community legislation and did not pave the way for a fourth stage in the evolution of Member State liability.

In conclusion, the principle of State liability, in its three stages of evolution, firstly enshrined in *Francovich* and later confirmed and expanded in *Brasserie/Factortame III* and *Köbler*, introduced a general right to damages for a breach of European law by Member States and its organs. Figure 6 visualizes this development, while outlining the operation of the principle.[836] However, in the end, especially due to the countless difficulties in establishing a sufficiently serious breach, the principle contributed more to the enforcement of European law than to achieve an effective protection of individual rights under it.

[836] See Figure 6: Overview on the Evolution of the Principle of Member State Liability, p. 125.

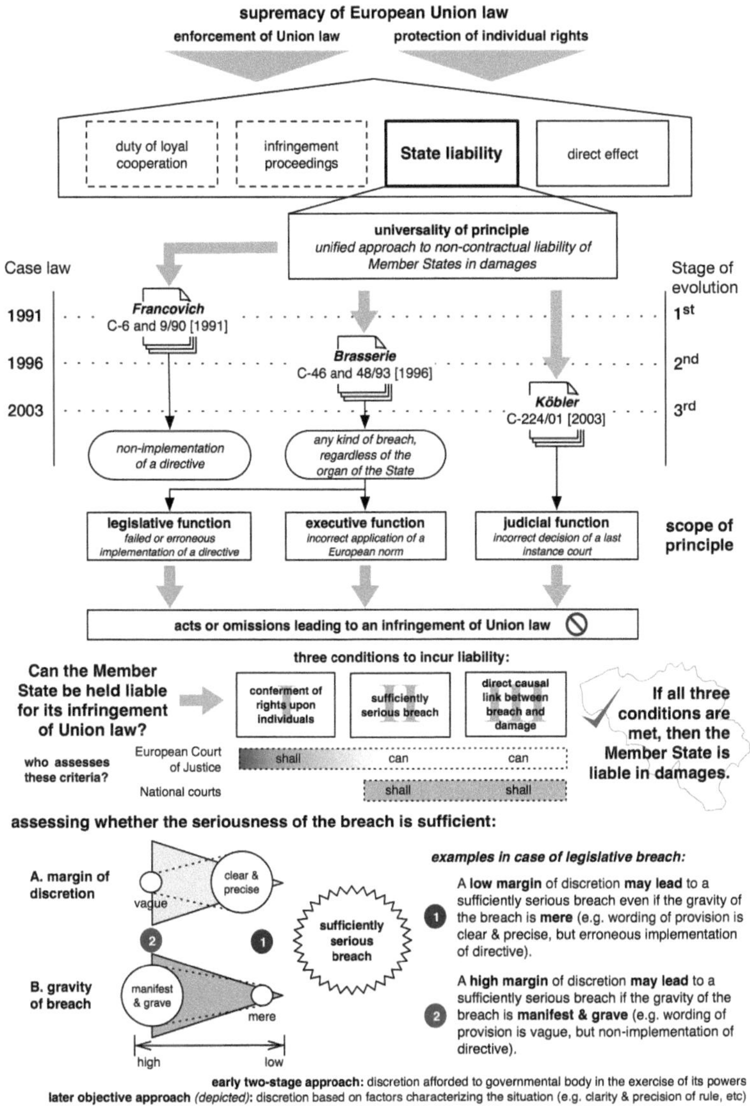

Figure 6: Overview on the Evolution of the Principle of Member State Liability

Figure 6. The development of the principle of State liability in case law goes through three stages. Each of the stages expands the scope of the principle. The operation of the principle inherently stays the same. A Member State is liable for its breach of European Union law if all three conditions are fulfilled.

Source: Own compilation.

Reference List

Articles in Periodicals:

Albors-Llorens, A. (2002). Courage v. Crehan: Judicial activism or consistent approach? *Cambridge Law Journal, 61*(1), 38–41.

Albors-Llorens, A. (2012). Remedies against EU institutions after Lisbon: An era of opportunity? *Cambridge Law Journal, 71*(3), 507–536.

Anagnostaras, G. (2001). The allocation of responsibility in State liability actions for breach of Community law: A modern Gordian knot? *European Law Review, 26*(2), 139–158.

Anagnostaras, G. (2006). Erroneous judgments and the prospect of damages: The scope of the principle of Governmental liability for judicial breaches. *European Law Review, 31*(5), 735–747.

Baeyens, A., & Goffin, T. (2009). ECJ 2009/01 Synthon BV v. Licensing Authority of the Department of Health, 16 October 2008 (C/452/06). *European Journal of Health Law, 16*, 105–109.

Bebr, G. (1992). Comment on Joined Cases C-6/90 and C-9/90 Francovich. *Common Market Law Review, 29*, 557–584.

Betlem, G. (1996). The king can do wrong: State liability for breach of European Community law in the Post-Francovich era. *Web Journal of Current Legal Issues, 4*. Retrieved from http://webjcli.ncl.ac.uk/1996/contents4.html

Betlem, G. (2005). Torts, a European ius commune and the private enforcement of Community law. *Cambridge Law Journal, 64*(1), 126–148.

Beutler, B. (2009). State liability for breaches of Community law by national courts: Is the requirement of a manifest infringement of the applicable law an insurmountable obstacle? *Common Market Law Review, 46*, 773–804.

Breuer, M. (2004). State liability for judicial wrongs and Community law: the case of Gerhard Köbler v. Austria. *European Law Review, 29*(2), 243–254.

Caranta, R. (1993). Governmental liability after Francovich. *Cambridge Law Journal, 52*(2), 272–297.

Caranta, R. (1995). Judicial protection against Member States: A new jus commune takes shape. *Common Market Law Review, 32*, 703–726.

Convery, J. (1997). State liability in the United Kingdom after Brasserie du Pêcheur. *Common Market Law Review, 34*, 603–634.

Davies, A. (2012). State liability for judicial decisions in European Union and international law. *International and Comparative Law Quarterly, 61*(3), 585–611.

Drake, S. (2006). Scope of Courage and the principle of "individual liability" for damages: Further development of the principle of effective judicial protection by the Court of Justice. *European Law Review, 31(6)*, 841–864.

Granger, M.-P. F. (2007). National applications of Francovich and the construction of a European administrative jus commune. *European Law Review, 32*(2), 157–192.

Groussot, X., & Minssen, T. (2007). Res judicata in the Court of Justice case-law. *European Constitutional Law Review, 3*(3), 385–417.

Gutman, K. (2011). The evolution of the action for damages against the European Union and its place in the system of judicial protection. *Common Market Law Review, 48*, 695–750.

Hanft, J. E. (1991). Francovich and Bonifaci v. Italy: EEC Member State liability for failure to implement Community directives. *Fordham International Law Journal, 15*(4), 1237–1274.

Harlow, C. (1996). Francovich and the problem of the disobedient State. *European Law Journal, 2*(3), 199–225.

Hilson, C. (2005). The role of discretion in EC law on non-contractual liability. *Common Market Law Review, 42*, 677–695.

Krümmel, T., & D'Sa, R. M. (2009). Implementation by German courts of the jurisprudence of the European Court of Justice on State liability for breach of Community law as developed in Francovich and subsequent cases. *European Business Law Review, 20*(2), 274–286.

Lane, R. (1996). The fisherman's tale: National liability for breaches of Community law. *Edinburgh Law Review, 1*(1), 91–105.

Lenaerts, K. (2003). Interlocking legal orders in the European Union and comparative law. *International and Comparative Law Quarterly, 52*, 873–906.

Lowry, A. (2004). Suing the State for breaches of Community law by the Supreme Court. *The Bar Review, 9*(3), 107–111.

Millarg, E. (1977). Keine Staatshaftung für gemeinschaftswidrige Gesetzgebung? *Zeitschrift für Rechtspolitik, 10*, 224–226.

Nassimpian, D. (2007). And we keep on meeting: (De)fragmenting State liability. *European Law Review, 32*(6), 819–838.

Oliver, P. (1997). Cases C-46/93 and C-48/93 Brasserie du Pêcheur v. Germany, and The Queen v. Secretary of State for Transport ex parte Factortame [1996] ECR I-1029. *Common Market Law Review, 34*, 635–658.

Oliver, P. (1997b). Case C-392/93 The Queen v. Her Majesty's Treasury ex parte British Telecommunications [1996] ECR I-1631. *Common Market Law Review, 34*, 658–680.

Prechal, S. (1990). Remedies after Marshall. *Common Market Law Review, 27*, 451–473.

Prechal, S. (2006b). Member State liability and direct effect: What's the difference after all? *European Business Law Review, 17*(2), 299–316.

Puder, M. (2000). Phantom menace or new hope: Member State public tort liability after the double-bladed light saber duel between the European Court of Justice and the German Bundesgerichtshof in Brasserie du Pêcheur. *Vanderbilt Journal of Transnational Law, 33*, 311–370.

Rihs, G., & Steiner, A.-Z. (2013). "Hinreichend qualifizierter Verstoß" als neue materielle Voraussetzung für Schadensersatzansprüche (Teil 1). *Zeitschrift für Vergaberecht und Bauvertragsrecht, 4*, 138–143.

Ross, M. (1993). Beyond Francovich. *The Modern Law Review, 56*(1), 55–73.

Ruffert, M. (2007). Case C-173/03 Traghetti del Mediterraneo SpA in Liquidation v. Italian Republic, Judgment of the Court (Great Chamber) of 13 June 2006. *Common Market Law Review, 44*, 479–500.

Scherr, K. M. (2012). Comparative aspects of the application of the principle of State liability for judicial breaches. *Europäische Rechtsakademie Forum, 12*, 565–588.

Tallberg, J. (2000). Supranational influence in EU enforcement: The ECJ and the principle of State liability. *Journal of European Public Policy, 7*(1), 104–121.

Tomkin, J. (2012). Case C-243/09, Günter Fuß, Judgment of the Court of Justice (Second Chamber) of 14 October 2010, nyr; Case C-429/09, Günter Fuß, Judgment of the Court of Justice (Second Chamber) of 25 November 2010, nyr. *Common Market Law Review, 49*, 1423–1442.

Tridimas, T. (1996). Member State liability in damages. *The Cambridge Law Journal, 55*, 412–415.

Tridimas, T. (2001). Liability for breach of Community law: Growing up and mellowing down? *Common Market Law Review, 38*, 301–332.

Uecker, R. (1994). Francovich and beyond: A German perspective. *European Business Law Review, 5*(12), 286–291.

Vaitkevičiūtė, A. (2011). Member States liability in damages for the breach of European legal basis and conditions for liability. *Jurisprudence, 18*(1), 49–68.

Van Gerven, W. (1996). Bridging the unbridgeable: Community and national tort laws after Francovich and Brasserie. *International and Comparative Law Quarterly, 45*, 507–544

Wattel, P. J. (2004). Köbler, CILFIT and Welthgrove: We can't go on meeting like this. *Common Market Law Review, 41*, 177–190.

Wooldridge, F., & D'Sa, R. M. (1996). ECJ decides Factortame (No 3) and Brasserie du Pêcheur. *European Business Law Review, 7*(6), 161–167.

Zingales, N. (2010). Member State liability vs. national procedural autonomy: What rules for judicial breach of EU Law? *German Law Journal, 11*(4), 419–438.

<u>Books:</u>

Aalto, P. (2011). *Public Liability in EU Law: Brasserie, Bergaderm and beyond*. Oxford: Hart Publishing.

Arnull, A. (2000). The action for annulment: A case of double standards? In D. O'Keefe (Ed.), *Judicial Review in European Union Law: Volume 1* (pp. 177–190). The Hague: Kluwer Law International.

Barav, A. (1988). Damages in the domestic courts for breach of Community law by national public authorities. In H. Schermers, T. Heukels, & P. Mead (Eds.), *Non-contractual liability of the European Communities* (pp. 149–168). Dordrecht: Kluwer Academic Publishers.

Basedow, J. (2007). Jurisdiction and choice of law. In J. Basedow (Ed.), *Private enforcement of EC competition law* (pp. 229–254). Alphen aan den Rijn: Kluwer Law International.

Bebr, G. (1994). Court of Justice: Judicial protection and the rule of law. In D. Curtin, & T. Heukels (Eds.), *Institutional dynamics of European integration: Volume II* (pp. 303–334). Dordrecht: Kluwer Academic Publishers.

Beck, G. (2012). *The legal reasoning of the Court of Justice of the EU*. Oxford and Portland, Oregon: Hart Publishing.

Caranta, R. (2008). On discretion. In S. Prechal, & B. van Roermund (Eds.), *The coherence of EU law: The search for unity in divergent concepts* (pp. 185–216). Oxford: Oxford University Press.

Chalmers, D., Davies, G., & Monti, G. (2010). *European Union law: Cases and materials* (2nd ed.). Cambridge: Cambridge University Press.

Conant, L. (2012). Compliance and what EU Member States make of it. In M. Cremona (Ed.), *Compliance and the enforcement of EU law* (pp. 1–30). Oxford: Oxford University Press.

Craig, P. (1998). The Domestic Liability of Public Authorities in Damages: Lessons from the European Community? In J. Beatson, & T. Tridimas (Eds.), *New directions in European public law* (pp. 75–90). Oxford: Hart Publishing.

Craig, P. (2012). *EU administrative law* (2nd ed.). Oxford: Oxford University Press.

Craig, P., & de Búrca, G. (2011). *EU law – Text, cases and material* (5th ed.). Oxford: Oxford University Press.

De Witte, B. (2011). Direct effect, primacy and the nature of the legal order. In P. Craig, & G. de Búrca (Eds.), *The evolution of EU law* (2nd ed.) (pp. 323–406). Oxford: Oxford University Press.

Dougan, M. (2002). Enforcing the single market: The judicial harmonisation of national remedies and procedural rules. In C. Barnard, & J. Scott (Eds.), *The law of the single European market: Unpacking the premises* (pp. 153–180). Oxford: Hart Publishing.

Dougan, M. (2004). National remedies before the Court Of Justice - Issues of harmonisation and differentiation. Oxford and Portland, Oregon: Hart Publishing.

Dougan, M. (2004b). What is the point of Francovich? In T. Tridimas, & P. Nebbia (Eds.), *European Union law for the twenty-first century: Rethinking the new legal order, Volume 1* (pp. 239–258). Oxford: Hart Publishing.

Dougan, M. (2011). Remedies and procedures for enforcing Union law. In P. Craig, & G. de Búrca (Eds.), *The evolution of EU law* (2nd ed.) (pp. 407–438). Oxford: Oxford University Press.

Dougan, M. (2012). From the velvet glove to the iron fist: Criminal sanctions for the enforcement of EU law. In M. Cremona (Ed.), *Compliance and the enforcement of EU law* (pp. 74–131). Oxford: Oxford University Press.

Douglas-Scott, S. (2002). *Constitutional law of the European Union.* Essex: Pearson Education Limited.

Dourado, A. P. (2008). Is it acte clair? General report on the role played by CILFIT in direct taxation. In A. P. Dourado, & R. da Palma Borges (Eds.), *The acte clair in EC direct tax law* (pp. 13–70). Amsterdam: IBFD.

Edward, D., & Lane, R. (2013). *Edward and Lane on European Union law.* Cheltenham: Edward Elgar Publishing Limited.

Foster, N. (2013). *Questions & answers EU law 2013 and 2014* (9th ed.). Oxford: Oxford University Press.

Harlow, C., & Rawlings, R. (2010). *Law and administration* (3rd ed.). Cambridge: Cambridge University Press.

Hartley, T.C. (2007). *The foundations of European Community law: An introduction to the constitutional and administrative law of the European Community* (6th ed.). Oxford: Oxford University Press.

Hess, B. (2012). Procedural harmonisation in a European context. In X. E. Kramer, & C. H. van Rhee (Eds.), *Civil litigation in a globalising world* (pp. 159–174). The Hague: T. M. C. Asser Press.

Horspool, M., & Humphreys, M. (2006). *European Union law* (4th ed.). Oxford: Oxford University Press.

Jones, A., & Sufrin, B. (2008). *EC Competition Law: Texts, Cases and Materials* (3rd ed.). Oxford: Oxford University Press.

Kapteyn, P. J. G., & VerLoren Van Themaat, P. (2008). *The law of the European Union and European Communities* (4th ed.). Alphen aan den Rijn: Kluwer Law International.

Kaczorowska, A. (2013). *European Union law* (3rd ed.). New York: Routledge.

Kelemen, R. D. (2004). *The rules of federalism: Institutions and regulatory politics in the EU and beyond*. Cambridge, Massachusetts: Harvard University Press.

Kent, P. (2008). *Law of the European Union* (4th ed.). Harlow: Pearson Education Limited.

Komárek, J. (2012). Reasoning with previous decisions. In M. Adams, & J. Bomhoff (Eds.), *Practice and theory in comparative law* (pp. 49–73). Cambridge: Cambridge University Press.

Leczykiewicz, D. (2010). Private party liability in EU law: In search of the general regime. In C. Barnard, & O. Odudu (Eds.), *The Cambridge Yearbook of European Legal Studies 2009-2010* (pp. 257–282). Oxford: Hart Publishing.

Lee, I. (2000). *In search of a theory of State liability in the European Union*. Cambridge: Harvard Law School.

Lenaerts, K., & Van Nuffel, P. (2011). *European Union law* (3rd ed.). London: Sweet & Maxwell.

Prechal, S. (1995). *Directives in European Community law: A study of directives and their enforcement in national courts*. Oxford: Clarendon Press.

Prechal, S. (2006). *Directives in EC law* (2nd ed.). Oxford: Oxford University Press.

Prechal, S. (2008). Protection of rights: How far? In S. Prechal, & B. van Roermund (Eds.), *The coherence of EU law: The search for unity in divergent concepts* (pp. 155–182). Oxford: Oxford University Press.

Reich, N. (2005). *Understanding EU law*. Oxford: Hart Publishing.

Schermers, H., & Waelbroeck, D. (2001). *Judicial protection in the European Union* (6th ed.). The Hague/London/New York: Kluwer Law International.

Schütze, R. (2012). *European constitutional law*. Cambridge: Cambridge University Press.

Streinz, R. (2012). *Europarecht* (9th ed.). Heidelberg/München/Landsberg/Frechen/ Hamburg: C.F. Müller.

Tridimas, T. (1998). Member State liability in damages for breach of Community law: An assessment of the case law. In J. Beatson, & T. Tridimas (Eds.), *New directions in European public law* (pp. 11–34). Oxford: Hart Publishing.

Tridimas, T. (2007). State liability for judicial acts - Remedies unlimited? In P. Demaret, I. Govaere, & D. Hanf (Eds.), *Dynamiques juridiques européennes* (pp. 147–160). Brussels: Peter Lang – International Academic Publishers.

Tridimas, T. (2012). Bifurcated justice: The dual chapter of judicial protection in EU law. In Court of Justice of the European Union (Ed.), *The Court of Justice and the construction of Europe: Analyses and perspectives on sixty years of case-law* (pp. 367–380). The Hague: T.M.C. Asser Press.

Türk, A. (2009). *Judicial review in EU law*. Cheltenham: Edward Elgar Publishing Limited.

Van Dam, C. (2013). *European tort law* (2nd ed.). Oxford: Oxford University Press.

Van Gerven, W. (2007). Private enforcement of EC competition rules in the ECJ – Courage v. Crehan and the way ahead. In J. Basedow (Ed.), *Private enforcement of EC competition law* (pp. 19–28). Alphen aan den Rijn: Kluwer Law International.

Weatherill, S. (2010). *Cases and materials on EU law* (9th ed.). Oxford: Oxford University Press.

Widdershoven, R. (2002). European administrative law. In R. Seerden, & F. Stroink (Eds.), *Administrative law of the European Union, its Member States and the United States* (pp. 259–306). Antwerpen-Groningen: Intersentia Uitgevers.

Wolf, C. (1999). *Die Staatshaftung der Bundesrepublik Deutschland und der Französischen Republik für Verstöße gegen das Europäische Gemeinschaftsrecht*. Berlin: Dunker & Humblot.

Wurmnest, W., & Heinze, C. (2011). General principles of tort law in the jurisprudence of the European Court of Justice. In R. Schulze (Ed.), *Compensation of private losses: The evolution of torts in European business law* (pp. 39–68). Munich: Sellier European Law Publishers GmbH.

<u>Publications by the European Commission:</u>

Commission of the European Communities. (1975). *Reports on European Union: European Parliament, Court of Justice, Economic and Social Committee*. Bulletin of the European Communities Supplement, 9/75. Brussels: Commission of the European Communities.

Commission of the European Communities. (1991). *Intergovernmental Conferences: Contributions by the Commission*. Bulletin of the European Communities Supplement, 2/91. Brussels/Luxembourg: Office for Official Publications of the European Communities.

European Union, European Commission. (2009). *Case law of the Court of Justice of the European Union connected with claims for damages relating to breaches of EU law by Member States*. Retrieved July 29, 2013, from http://ec.europa.eu/eu_law/infringements/pdf/jur_09_30385_en.pdf

<u>Other sources:</u>

Kondas, M. (2008, October 20). Pre-Brasserie applications by the ECJ. Retrieved July 29, 2013, from http://www.asser.nl/upload/eel-webroot/www/documents/cms_eel_id179_1_PreBrasserie.pdf

Vedder, H. (2013, March 27). Leth: Court rules out Francovich claim on the basis of the Environmental Impact Assessment Directive [Web log post]. Retrieved July 29, 2013, from http://europeanlawblog.eu/?p=1630

Appendices

Numerical Table of European Cases

Alphabetical Table of European Cases

Table of Opinions of Advocate Generals

Table of Cases under National Law

United Kingdom

Table of Treaties

Treaty establishing the European Coal and Steel Community (ECSC)

Treaty establishing the European Economic Community (EEC)

Treaty establishing the European Community (TEC)

Treaty on European Union (TEU)

Treaty on the Functioning of the European Union (TFEU)

Table of European Union and Community Acts

Decisions

Directives

Table of Acts under National Law

Germany

Italy

United Kingdom

MIX
Papier aus verantwortungsvollen Quellen
Paper from responsible sources
FSC® C105338

If you have any concerns about our products,
you can contact us on
ProductSafety@springernature.com

In case Publisher is established outside the EU,
the EU authorized representative is:
Springer Nature Customer Service Center GmbH
Europaplatz 3, 69115 Heidelberg, Germany

Printed by Libri Plureos GmbH
in Hamburg, Germany